Praise for

En Garde: Crossing the stream of life

I was fortunate to have worked with Todd before I retired from NCIS, where I had the privilege of being both his supervisor and, most importantly, his friend. Throughout our time together, Todd consistently demonstrated a strong work ethic and a positive attitude, regardless of the task at hand. I often found myself wondering how he managed to stay focused and positive, even during challenging times and difficult investigations.

After reading *En Garde*, I finally understood how Todd managed to maintain his determination and clarity. This book reveals that despite the struggles and hardships we all face, God has a plan for each of us—just as He had a plan for Todd's life. Todd's journey shows that we may experience many setbacks, but God is always there to lift us up and help us move forward. *En Garde* is an emotional journey that reminds us that life is full of ups and downs, both in our personal lives and relationships. However, by trusting in God, we can navigate these challenges, and over time, things will work out.

The book also serves as a powerful guide for understanding and coping with both losses and wins. It teaches us how to respond to life's goals when we are met with adversity, and provides wisdom on overcoming obstacles. One of the most impactful aspects of the book is the activity section at the end of each chapter. Each section encourages readers to reflect on the material and apply it to their own lives, either individually or as part of a group discussion. It offers an invaluable opportunity to process the lessons and grow.

One powerful lesson from *En Garde* that especially resonated with me was these words: "Free yourself from living in regret." This sentiment reverberates throughout the book, urging readers to release the weight of past mistakes and embrace the journey ahead. The book is a profound reminder that no matter the struggles we face in life, having God's guidance and the support of our loved ones makes all the difference in overcoming adversity and finding peace Todd's story and the lessons in *En Garde* demonstrate that with hard work, patience, the support of family, and—most importantly—trusting in God, we can face life's challenges and emerge stronger than ever.

—Fidel Arroyo, Supervisory Special Agent (SSA), NCIS, Retired

***

As his first cousin, I have known Todd Griffee all of his life. In *En Garde*, Todd's grit, tenacity and faith are on full display. By baring his soul, and sharing his challenges and personal loss, Todd has provided us with the tools to deal with life's difficulties, and recognize God's grace and intervention. Through the two-part story of his life, Todd gives us peace and comfort in knowing that we are not alone. Todd's end-of-chapter Activities help the reader learn from his experiences and give them a way to prayerfully cope with adversity in their own life.

—Andrew A. Guljas, Facilities Management Coordinator, *Roman Catholic Diocese of Lafayette; Notre Dame Class of 1984*

***

In *En Garde*, Todd Griffee introduces faith into real-life events. Whether life is going well or hitting some major potholes, faith is central to the life lessons being learned. Todd includes journaling nudges with each chapter so the reader can see how their reality can be enlightened by the same life lessons. This book would be great for a small group to work through together or for an individual who is seeking to grow in connecting their faith and life.

—**Rev. Pamela Thiede**, Vicar, *Calumet Episcopal Ministry Partnership*

EN GARDE

Crossing the stream of life

Todd Griffee

Published by KHARIS PUBLISHING, an imprint of KHARIS MEDIA LLC.

Copyright © 2025 Todd Griffee

ISBN-13: 978-1-63746-354-3

ISBN-10: 1-63746-354-5

Library of Congress Control Number: 2025945062

All rights reserved. This book or parts thereof may not be reproduced in any form, stored in a retrieval system, or transmitted in any form by any means - electronic, mechanical, photocopy, recording, or otherwise - without prior written permission of the publisher, except as provided by United States of America copyright law.

All KHARIS PUBLISHING products are available at special quantity discounts for bulk purchases for sales promotions, premiums, fund-raising, and educational needs. For details, contact:

Kharis Media LLC
Tel: 1-630-909-3405
support@kharispublishing.com
www.kharispublishing.com

Table of Contents

Introduction xi

Chapter 1: Bargaining Between A Relationship and Vocation 17

Chapter 2: Ever Consider a Career in Southern Law Enforcement 22

Chapter 3: Beat Your Head Against the Wall, and Eventually the Wall Will Break 28

Chapter 4: Try A Different Path 35

Chapter 5: Seize The Opportunity 42

Chapter 6: Never Routine 48

Chapter 7: Sacrifices 55

Chapter 8: Hero to Zero 59

Chapter 9: Judged by 12 67

Chapter 10: Vindication 73

Chapter 11: Back in the Saddle 78

Chapter 12: Midnights in the Jail 81

Chapter 13: A Tale of Two Pubs 85

Chapter 14: A String of Burning Bushes 97

Chapter 15: Stuck 103

Chapter 16: The Unthinkable 107

Chapter 17: A New Plan 111

Chapter 18: Run for Office 115

Chapter 19: Court Ordered into Law Enforcement 121

Chapter 20: Life in Virginia 127

Chapter 21: Get Me Home 131

Chapter 22: Life at Crane 135

Chapter 23: New Beginnings 139

Chapter 24: Navy CID 143

Chapter 25: Finally Made it to the Big Leagues 148

Chapter 26: NCIS Advancement and Touché 153

Conclusion *156*

Final Thoughts *157*

Prayer *159*

About Kharis Publishing: *161*

This book is dedicated to my loving wife, Bonnie Jo, who has been my inspiration and muse in the adventure of becoming an author. It was her insistence, support, and guidance which gave me the courage to forge forward.

I would also like to dedicate this book to those who are still suffering from ravages of life. May you have hope God will deliver you from your pain and to find God's plan for your life.

Introduction

Purpose of En Garde: Crossing the Stream of Life

En Garde is a continuation of Touché; a Notre Dame All-American fencer's spiritual guide to success©. En Garde demonstrates how the goal setting formula in Touché was used over and over with great success, even under very trying circumstances. Touché concluded with my graduation from Notre Dame. The focus of Touché was to lay the ground work for the basic lessons I learned and applied to successfully graduate from Notre Dame. Touché left one goal unfulfilled – becoming a federal agent. Touché started with my discovery of my vocation - becoming a G-Man, and En Garde tells the twisted journey seeking that goal. En Garde covers the timeline from graduating Notre Dame until the present time. Thirty-six years of trials, tribulations, and triumphs were negotiated utilizing the principles outlined in Touché. Even the publication of Touché and my recent NCIS successes are direct results of the Touché method. The life lessons presented in Touché are robust, reliable, and rewarding. En Garde differs from Touché in that it is more than just goal setting and trouble shooting. En Garde covers many trials—some resulting in great loss—and the purpose is deeper than just overcoming an adversity. It is sharing my stories of loss to provide hope to others, because they will see they are not alone in their suffering.

I was told many years ago, one of the reasons we humans go through trauma and loss is to share with other sufferers that they are not alone. Death, divorce, financial devastation, loss of a business, bankruptcy, loss of an election, loss of a job, loss of a house, alcohol abuse, and prosecution are all major life changing events which cause immense amounts of stress on an individual. I am not sharing my stories of loss to "one-up" anyone or to seek sympathy. I am not sharing my shortcomings to take my moral inventory in front of the entire world. I am sharing this saga so those who are suffering can have faith that God will provide the miracle healing, just as He did for me. Just like the major message in Touché, if God can work miracles in my life, have faith, God can work miracles in your life!

Explanation of En Garde; Crossing the stream of life

Of course, life can be beautiful, wonderful, and fulfilling, but rarely do people need assistance with enjoying the joys of this life. Life can be brutal. It can knock you down and hit you so hard that you cannot even imagine trying to pick yourself up again. This is where people lose hope, and feel alone and dejected. This is where they need the helping message of "be on the ready." In other words, be on the guard, aka en garde in French. En garde is the command to be ready in a fencing bout, which carries over the fencing motif of Touché. My hope for En Garde is for the reader to learn the required lessons so they can be ready when trouble looms their way.

The subtitle, Crossing the stream of life, refers to one of Notre Dame Fencing Coach DeCicco's life lessons, which I shared in Touché. When I was worried about my future, Coach, with his infinite wisdom, told me a story about crossing a stream. He said if you focus too much on the other side, you will slide off the slippery stones you are using to cross the stream. If you only focus on the single slippery stone you are on, you will never see how to cross the stream. The key is to keep an eye on the stone you are on, look at the next stone, make the step, and look up occasionally to make sure you are heading in the right direction. Such it is with life. I have used this analogy tirelessly throughout my life.

No Sour Grapes

I want to emphasize, when I discuss my difficulties, there are no "sour grapes." This is not a pity party or a solicitation for attention. The purpose is to give the reader the opportunity to learn from real and tangible obstacles in life. The bigger the obstacle, the bigger the required miracle to overcome it. It was emotionally exhausting writing this book. The amount of loss and heartache was so overwhelming, it opened old wounds as I relived endless failures and trauma. There were times when I broke down crying remembering pain, which had been long forgotten. I had several family members read the manuscript for their input and they were overwhelmed with the negativity of the content. By the time the reader gets to the middle of the book, it appears little hope is left. Please, I encourage you to forge on because it is out of that darkness, where God's promises of wanting me to be happy, joyful, and free come to fruition. This is not about me and look at what a great job I did, or how strong I was to take those beatings and continue to move forward. This is about God being a show off and working miracles in a flawed sinner's life. God enjoys using flawed people for His missions.

Villains

En Garde does not focus on the villains in these obstacles. In a society where everyone is so fascinated with the serial killer, yet cannot name the countless victims, I do not wish to name the villains because they are not the focus of my story. The focus is God miraculously guiding me through the negotiation of my troubles. I changed the names of many villains and potential villains, just for that reason. I also changed the names of some individuals because it is not fair to make my cross easier to bear by making someone else's cross heavier. There are always two sides to every story and it is not my purpose to plead my case to justify my actions. There are also examples of what I did to put myself into a position to be hurt. Finally, sometimes, life happens on life's terms and there are no villains.

The Mother of My Children

When I solicited feedback from my children concerning the rough manuscript, they felt obligated to take their mother's side in regard to the divorce and were very protective of her. I thought my treatment of her in the rough manuscript was fair because I did not address her shortcomings. I only addressed my reactions to her and my shortcomings. The book is about my failings and trials and I how I struggled to grow spiritually through those experiences. Never once did I attempt to rationalize or justify my position with the mother of my children, to plead my case.

The children also voiced how reading the manuscript opened old wounds, and they discussed their resentments of me which they were forced to work through. They also made it known they were embarrassed by the divorce and did not want to air the family's dirty laundry because it was nobody else's business.

This placed me in a dilemma; I believed my responsibility is to the reader, who may be comforted or inspired by trials in my life. Yet, I want my children to know I respect their feelings, as well. As parents, we sacrifice so much, and it can be heartbreaking when those sacrifices are minimized by being resented and are seen as embarrassing. I believe writing from the heart is art, and art can be embarrassing because true art lets the audience view into the vulnerabilities of your very soul. This can be a very humbling experience, but a necessary one to invoke the intended emotional or intellectual response. I did my best to balance that goal with the desires of my children. They actually wanted their mother removed from the book, but I could not tell a large portion of my story without including her. I removed the names of my children and changed their mother's name to, "Michelle," in an attempt to respect their wishes.

The children wanted their mother to be remembered as a hard working mother, who loved her children dearly, and fought a courageous battle with cancer. For the record, I loved Michelle and she was a fantastic mother to our children. Despite our differences, we continued to co-parent and both sacrificed whatever was necessary to provide for the kids. On her deathbed, Michelle asked me to love the kids and asked all of us to never forget her.

Ambiguity of Alcohol Abuse

The reader might be wondering why I am vague when discussing the specifics of the alcohol abuse program, which was so instrumental in getting me sober nearly 24 years ago. The reason is because that specific organization forbids utilizing their name in the media or for use in a book such as this. The program is a recovery program of attraction, not promotion. If you are in need of alcohol treatment, please use the internet to locate a program in your area. They will be able to give you the required specifics of the program. En Garde is about God's miracles and less about the specific tools He used.

En Garde's Layout

The layout to En Garde is very similar to Touché. Each chapter concludes with a goal or lesson for reflection and space for the reader to make notes concerning the negotiation of their goals or dilemmas. En Garde is written either to read all at once, or with a different chapter read for a daily reflection. Please feel free to highlight, underline, or make notes on anything which would be of use to you. En Garde could also be utilized as the subject of a book/spiritual/leadership study group. Ultimately, the goal of En Garde is to provide readers with hope God will manifest miracles in their lives!

Chapter 1

Bargaining Between A Relationship and Vocation

Touché revealed how I discovered my vocation, and what means I went through for twelve years to work toward the goal of becoming a G-Man. The journey through Notre Dame was a rich and rewarding experience, which took a brutal toll. Balancing classes, studying, work, ROTC, and being a varsity athlete was a Herculean endeavor, and quite honestly, it was a miracle in itself. What I did not discuss in Touché were relationships because it did not have much bearing on the focus. It did have a focus on the rest of my life.

I had two primary love interests in college. The first was Cathy, whom I dated my sophomore year. Cathy was a Purdue student who eventually transferred to Notre Dame. She was incredibly smart. I had to study relentlessly to earn every mediocre grade I could get, but Cathy never had to study to get straight A's. We met when I had just decided not to drop out of school and was gaining great success in fencing due to seeing a sports psychologist. Things were looking up, and this new relationship was unlike anything I had ever experienced. I let my guard down and opened myself up like never before. It was a rewarding and fulfilling sensation. Then the unthinkable happened. Out of the blue, without warning, Cathy called me and advised me she was ending the relationship because she wanted to go back to an ex-boyfriend. I do not know what hurt more. The startling, unexpected delivery of the bad news, the end of a relationship I treasured, or the embarrassment of appearing the bloody fool. Whichever it was, my heart was ripped out. I felt physically sick to my stomach, my head was pounding with a massive headache, and I felt discarded like a piece of trash. This was my first major love and it was gone like a flash in the pan. Not knowing how to stop the physical, psychological, and emotional pain, I holed myself up in my room and drank myself silly. After two days of anguish, I removed myself from the confines of my room and told my mum the entire story. My mother was never one to mince words. She told me to snatch myself up and take pride in myself. She exclaimed that anyone who did not recognize my true potential and was quick to discard me was unworthy of my grief. Basically, she told me to suck it up, keep my chin up, and time would heal my heart, until I found the right girl. Days later, Cathy called me and apologized for the huge mistake she had made. She said she regretted it terribly, wanted me to forgive her, and to resume the relationship. Mum had made it clear: Under no circumstances can I go back to her! If she did it once, she'll do it again. I accepted my mother's advice as gospel and told Cathy renewing the relationship was not possible.

This leads to love interest number two – Theresa. Theresa was a senior in high school when we met working at the

University Club in my junior year. I had been so busy with school and extracurricular activities that I'd had little time for pursuing a serious relationship since Cathy. Theresa and I started dating and things progressed at a slower, steadier pace than with Cathy. Theresa started St. Mary's College my senior year and we talked of marriage when she graduated. This is when the bargaining started. If you are familiar with the works, of Dr. Elisabeth Kubler-Ross, involving the five stages of grief, then you know "bargaining" is one of those stages. As Theresa and I started mapping out our future, red flags started popping up. Theresa made it clear she did not want to leave the area and my wanting to be a federal agent would require me to relocate. I was so terrified of losing this relationship, due to the pain I experienced losing Cathy that I started bargaining away my vocation. I told her I could get into a local police department and stay locally. She never really objected to the notion, but she never really accepted it. I stuck my head in the sand, ignored it, and kept planning our future without a proper discussion. When I graduated from Notre Dame, I bought Theresa a diamond ring and proposed, but not without asking her father's consent first. She accepted the proposal and seemed genuinely excited so I continued planning. I was leaving for my Army Military Police Officer Basic Course at Ft. McClellan, AL in August so in the meantime I worked in her father's hardware store. A few weeks after the proposal, Theresa's father received a phone call and told me I had to rush home for an emergency. Upon arrival, I found Mum and Theresa sitting at the kitchen table. What was the emergency? Theresa gave back my ring and broke off the engagement. She stated her parents gave her an ultimatum. Break up with me or they would not pay for her college. They did not want their daughter married to a police officer. Once again, I tried the ridiculous bargaining by stating

I would pay for her college. Her response was an honest one. Theresa said she did not want to be married to a police officer. Once again, I felt the embarrassment and anguish of a lost love. After some grieving, I was able to clear my head and see the signs were there all along. This woman did not want to be a part of my life as long as it involved law enforcement. At least she was honest about it. This also meant she loved me conditionally and I was so blinded, I nearly bargained away my vocation for someone who only loved me conditionally. My father stepped in and provided further insight into not compromising my goals for someone who was not willing to appreciate those goals. I took those lessons and my parents' advice to heart and was more determined than ever not to let anything get in the way of my calling.

Activity

As we struggle to find our purpose and achieve our goals, we are always being tested with bargaining. Sometimes we are tired and seek an easier path or we are fear-driven and cannot part with an unfulfilling relationship. Sometimes compromise is a necessity because you might have obligations like children or caring for a sick family member, which gives you no real choice. But often there are choices. The key is to weigh the options in a healthy manner to determine the advantages of either action. Regardless of whether the compromise is justified or not, it will lead to resentment and anguish later down the road. In Touché, I related the experiences of patrons at my father's tavern when I was growing up. There were countless stories of missed opportunities and lost love. For example, I heard stories where someone had a try out for a major league baseball team, but did not follow through because he had gotten his girlfriend pregnant. There was the story of the guy whose wife was the love of his life, yet she ran away with her high school sweetheart. There was the story of the guy who had a tryout with the Chicago Bears™ but did not go because he had to work to support his family. There were endless heartbreaking stories of lost purpose. These people were not only stuck in life, but they were also stuck in time. They would drink and talk endlessly about their past. They were unable to move on and have conversations about the glories of living today. Understand the effects compromise and bargaining can have on life. In this activity, write down situations where you have bargained and compromised. What did it cost you? Are you still on track to a fulfilling life? Remember, no matter how far off the road you get, there is hope you can arrive at your destination.

_____
_____
_____
_____
_____
_____
_____
_____
_____
_____
_____
_____
_____
_____
_____
_____

Chapter 2

Ever Consider a Career in Southern Law Enforcement

After the breakup with Theresa, I worked in a buddy's factory until I left for army training. I was excited about the upcoming training and to see the southeastern United States. I had never been there, but would eventually fall in love with this area of the country. The people were a little standoffish at first, until they got to know you. Then they were great friends. The people were very courteous and respectful and the rolling hills of Alabama were gorgeous. The weather was fantastic! I arrived with a new level of commitment to my vocation and knew the training I received in the Army would be advantageous. I studied hard and worked hard. Some of the training was quite rigorous but I threw myself into it and pushed myself to succeed. Prior to Christmas, a classmate received a flyer from Sarasota Police Department. They were doing all of their testing and interviewing over a single weekend after we were scheduled to graduate. My friend wanted to become a Pennsylvania trooper and I wanted to become a Fed. The competition for law enforcement jobs during this period of time was extreme. We both realized this new opportunity might give us an advantage by obtaining some local law enforcement experience. With nothing keeping me tied to home, this sounded like an exciting adventure, so we planned on moving to Florida after graduation.

I went home during Christmas leave and all of my friends were either out of town or busy. I was determined to do something for New Year's and ended up going out with Cathy. It was a nice date, where we buried the hatchet. A couple of weeks after our date, I received a letter from Cathy. She told me how she never stopped loving me, what a huge mistake she made, and asked me to marry her. I was taken aback. I did not see this coming and gave the proposal some serious consideration. I did care for her, but I could not get my mum's words out of my head. The tie breaker in my decision was the bargaining lesson I learned in the break up with Theresa. I had to be true to my vocation and continue with my plans of seeking a police job in Florida. I wrote Cathy and kindly explained my decision. We remained on friendly terms, but never attempted to develop a relationship afterwards.

After graduation, my friend and I arrived in Sarasota. We where informed the weekend of interviewing and testing was cancelled. That was a punch to the stomach. I needed a job so I was hired to sell encyclopedias. I sold three sets, and never received a check. What a scam. So I moved on and ended up working as a manager in a hardware store for $5.00 an hour. It was barely enough for me to keep my head above water so

I was always looking for a part time or better job. I met with the local DEA Office and asked them what was taking so long with my application, which I submitted immediately after Theresa broke up with me. They replied they changed their standards and my grade point average was a fraction of a fraction too low. Law enforcement had become extremely competitive. They told me I could have gone to some rinky dink junior college and got a 4.0 because where I went to school made no difference. I was punched in the stomach again. I had applied to ten other federal agencies and had heard nothing. The DEA office informed me I would need one year of law enforcement experience to continue so they called a local police department and put in a good word for me. I applied there and went in for my initial step and overheard the person in front of me being told his next step of the hiring cycle would be next week. When it was my turn, they told me the next step would be in six months. It was obvious they knew I was using them as a stepping stone to the Feds. Another punch to the stomach.

One night, a friend and I went to a local night club to chill out. I was in a silly mood and was not looking for a serious relationship. I observed this tall, well dressed, girl sitting with her friend. She had gorgeous, unusual colored blue eyes and a bobbed haircut, where the back was shorter than the front. Very 80s! Very cool! When I pointed her out to my buddy, he dared me to come up with a ridiculous line to make her laugh. Challenge accepted. Back in the 80s there was a well-known hair product commercial in which the male hair dresser walked up behind a woman, bounced her hair, and said, "Oh my God, who does your hair?" That is exactly what I did. I used the accent from the man in the commercial and used the very lines. I then told her I worked at that company's salon in Tampa and thought she looked smashing. The girl's name was

Michelle and she was so shocked, she could do nothing but laugh. A good laugh was had by all and I properly introduced myself and my friend and explained the ruse. We immediately hit it off. She told me she was an office manager for a local security company. The next day, I showed up to her office and applied for a security officer job. Michelle interviewed me for the job and hired me. Later that day, I sent her a dozen roses and asked her on a proper date. The job only paid $3.35 an hour, but it was enough to barely keep my head above water. Her father, who retired from the Air Force, became my supervisor so we got to know each other better. As Michelle and I got better acquainted, I learned she grew up in England most of her life and we had a lot in common. The relationship became serious and I disclosed the short-comings of my previous relationships. Michelle was quick to support me in my law enforcement quest and said she was used to moving with her family so she would go wherever I went. I took her home to meet my parents who really liked her. I explained to Michelle and my parents, I was not making enough money in Florida and would have move home for better income potential. My mother pulled me aside later and told me the only way we could stay there temporarily would be if we were married. Mum was a devote Catholic and her decision was beyond objection.

On the drive back to Florida, we stopped by an apple orchard, where I got on my knee and proposed to Michelle. She immediately accepted and we came up with a game plan. We could only afford one more month in Florida so we planned a small wedding for 01 JUL 1990. The day after the wedding, we headed to our next adventure in Michigan/Indiana.

Activity

The title of this chapter comes from the 80s TV show Miami Vice©, where Sonny asks Tubbs that very question. By the early 90s law enforcement opportunities were scarce and the competition was brutal. In this chapter, I was met with countless rejections and disappointments in achieving my vocation. I was also met with the temptation to compromise my vocation for a lost love. The lessons I learned were to be true to myself and stay focused on the mission, despite the failures. I had basically gone broke in Florida pursuing my dream, but was not defeated by the rejection. I was able to focus on my Army training, built networks with the Feds, gained a spouse who supported my dream, and had the ability to regroup and come up with a plan (B), which was moving back north. Rarely is a plan completed using plan (A) or plan (B). Sometimes you have to keep going to (X), (Y), and (Z). The important thing is to know yourself, learn from your mistakes, and keep planning.

Your activity for this chapter is to write down your reactions when you are presented with rejection or failure. Also write down members of your support system who will be there every step of the way. In this case it was my parents and Michelle who provided me with the courage not to be disappointed and to continue moving on.

Todd Griffee

Chapter 3

Beat Your Head Against the Wall, and Eventually the Wall Will Break

Michelle and I made it to my parents' house in Michigan, and they were gracious enough to permit us to stay with them until we found jobs and could find an apartment. Even though I missed Florida, the familiarity of home was comforting. Michelle sent out many resumes and I applied to many local police departments because I still needed that one year of law enforcement experience for DEA. In the meantime, I needed to find any job to get a cash flow. My dad's boss stopped by the house and said he needed someone to mix chemicals for his x-ray equipment company so I started work nearly as soon as I arrived. Then, a friend of Dad's from Jay's Lounge said his company needed a laborer for a road project. He was a heavy equipment operator and said they needed someone to chainsaw trees into small enough pieces to load on trucks for clearing the path for a new bypass highway. It paid $12.00 an hour for 12 hours a day. That was big money in 1990, so of course I said yes. The job had me start on a Friday. When I showed up, they gave me two old, tiny chainsaws. They would not stay running, got caught in the wood, the blades were dull, and were absolute junk. It was impossible for me to cut fast enough to keep up with the excavator loading the trucks. Both the excavator and truck drivers were yelling at me to speed it up, but I could not keep those saws running. The constant pulling on the starting cord began to blister my hands. They gave me some old gloves, but the inner seams were so rough, it cut my hands worse. Within a couple hours the blisters ripped open, and my hands started to bleed. At the end of the day, I had to fuel up all of the heavy equipment, which meant I got diesel fuel in my hands, which were transformed into raw hamburger. It was brutally hot that day and my nerves were shot from getting yelled at all day. I also was frustrated that I'd been unable to do a good job and felt like a miserable failure. When I got home, I told Michelle about my day and I told her I did not think I could take another day of torture. She looked at me and said I did not have a choice because we needed the money. She was correct. I made a vow to her to take care of her so I had to go back. I prayed like crazy and all day Sunday, I dreaded getting up at the crack of dawn Monday for another day of pain. When I got to the construction site, the foreman pulled up to me and told me he had a surprise for me. In the back of his truck were two, large, brand new chainsaws! I almost cried with excitement. Those saws went through those trees like butter. Within a couple hours I was caught up and by the end of the day, I was ahead of the machines. Within a week, I was so far ahead of the machines, I could not see them anymore. That torturous hell of a first day transformed into an enjoyable job spending time outdoors. Soon, I was miles ahead of the loading crew and the foreman approached me, asking if I could read blueprints because he heard I went to Notre Dame. I was able to read the prints so he made me a grade checker, which meant I told the machine operators where to cut dirt and where to put it. It was a cakewalk compared to chain sawing.

Then I received some good news on the law enforcement front. The Secret Service started me through their hiring process. Each step was a challenge and the polygraph was brutal. After four hours of interrogation, they finally told me I passed and they would not hesitate to follow me while responding to a dangerous situation. The last step was a meeting with the head of the office, who told me he never had a candidate go through the process this fast so he reassured me that it was a good sign. A local police department also started running me through their process and they gave me a polygraph, which was rinky dink compared to the Secret Service one. I was also waiting for another local police department to start their process and I submitted my application to the Indiana State Police (ISP). Things were looking up and these positive events provided me with the energy to keep working the construction job.

Winter was coming and the construction job boss told me I would be getting laid off soon. The blistering heat of summer quickly transformed into the bitter cold of winter. I still had not heard anything from any of the law enforcement jobs and I was laid off for the winter. I resorted to going door to door at retail stores, filling out applications. Bingo! The second store where I applied had a warehouse opening, and was able to start fairly quickly. It was not great money, but enough to get us through winter. Michelle was hired to be an office manager for an insurance adjuster, so that helped.

Spring rolled around and I was still waiting to hear from all of the agencies to which I'd applied. I kept hopeful and started the construction job again. Toward the end of the season, I was told by one agency they were not interested and they were extremely rude about it. I did not let that get me down because I still had hope Secret Service would come through. Finally, one day I received a letter from the Secret Service. This was it! This was my big break! My hands shook and I fumbled to get the envelope open. I opened it and it said Congratulations on being one of the few candidates to make it through our hiring process, but regretfully, we could only hire 30 agents and you have not been selected. Please apply again in a year. I was in shock! I felt the breath get ripped out of me and I felt like a mule kicked me in the chest. As crushed as I was, I knew I had to go to plan (B) so I went to the police department, which gave me the short polygraph. Now, one of the questions agencies like to ask you is have you applied with any other agencies. I was forced to tell them I had completed the process for Secret Service and was just waiting. My gut told me right then that they did not want me to use their agency as a stepping stone. When I spoke with the recruiter about where I was in the process, he informed me I failed the polygraph test. I laughed at him because I passed the Secret Service one. I asked if I could retake it and he said no because the chief did not think I was a good fit for the department.

Things were starting to look hopeless, when my step-grandfather, Grandpa Bob, died. He was a WWII veteran who was stationed in England. When I was young, he provided many colorful stories of his escapades. I was very close to him and worked on his farm with him often. I was devastated. Then, I received a letter from the ISP stating that due to the new Americans with Disabilities Act, they would be delaying their hiring for another year. I was beside myself and thought

I was going to drink myself silly at Grandpa Bob's wake. I felt empty and dejected. This is when life can be brutal and knock you down so hard you do not want to get up again.

Sometime after this, my grandmother, GG, said, "Maybe God is telling you He does not want you in law enforcement and that is why you have been met with so much rejection." In a moment of divine clarity, I responded, "Grand mum, if God did not want me in law enforcement, He would not have given me the desire in my heart. If I beat my head against the wall, the wall will break!"

Activity

This chapter discusses some extreme trials and losses I experienced providing for my family and on the quest for a law enforcement career. When I was at my lowest and my soul felt empty, God was able to inspire me to recognize that He placed that desire in my heart and it was my duty to continue the mission. I knew deep down, if I did not continue the journey, the regret would eat me alive and I would be trapped in a world of "what ifs." I did not want to be one of those people from the tavern who were trapped in their past.

Your activity is to write down your desires. What is deep in your heart that fuels your ambition? If life knocked you down, what passion would be so incredibly powerful it would force you to get up and try again? Identify the goals for which you are willing to sacrifice, suffer, and continue pursuing? Remember, times of great pain and suffering can decipher what is truly important to you and what is not. It is very similar to the difference between love and infatuation. With infatuation, when the going gets tough, you get going. With love, you will suffer for it to make it work!

Todd Griffee

En Garde: Crossing the stream of life

"Young LT" 1993, Fort Custer, MI.
(courtesy of 822 MP CO)

Chapter 4

Try A Different Path

After the discussion with GG, where I had the revelation God would not place the desire in my heart if He did not want me in law enforcement, I had no prospects on the table. In the early 90s, the competition for law enforcement positions was intense and the openings were few. Winter was coming and I knew I would be laid off from the construction job soon. This time I was better prepared for the lay off and started looking for jobs where I could utilize my education. I landed a job as a supervisor for a group home of mentally and physically disabled adults. It was work totally different than anything I had experienced before. At first, to see humans in such broken states was heartbreaking, but over time it instilled a new sense of compassion in my heart; not only for the clients, but for the dedicated staff who cared for them and trained them every day to become more independent. On the selfish side, the work was steady and the job paid enough for

Michelle and me to afford our rent and expenses without worry. Having the security of the income was nice for a change, but it did not extinguish the burning desire I had in my heart and it did not satisfy my thirst for adventure.

During this time, I had a successful career as an Army Reserve Officer as a Military Police (MP). One day I received an invitation to try-out for a Special Forces Reserve Unit. All I was missing was the language qualification. I took the Department of Defense language test for French, and failed. It was so hard, you would have had to be a French language teacher, who grew up in France, to pass. I do not think I could have passed the test in English. I did not let that deter me. After some research, I discovered if I scored high enough on the Defense Language Aptitude Battery (DLAB), I could get my language requirement waived and attend language school later. The DLAB test is a bogus language you learn as you progress through the test and that determines whether you have the aptitude to learn a foreign language. The problem was my company commander refused to approve my orders to attend the test. Back to the drawing board, until a weekend when the commander was absent and I was appointed the acting commander. My first order of business was signing my orders to attend the DLAB test! The DLAB test was very difficult, but I scored high enough to obtain the language waiver. I was then scheduled for an interview with the Special Forces unit. I was required to take an Army Physical Fitness Test (APFT), followed by an interview. The APFT was hideous. I did over 70 pushups and they said I only did 13 so I failed. I did over 100 sit-ups and was told I only did 19 so I failed. I failed the run as well. I was confused, but was determined to keep a military bearing and a positive attitude. I went into the interview with the attitude of having passed the APFT. The interview went very well and the Captain said

"Welcome aboard!" The lesson here was an important one and I have held onto it for the rest of my life. They said I failed the APFT. Most people would have said, "Oh, I failed. I'm leaving now." They would have quit because they were told they failed. The real test here was, am I going to quit when the chips were down? The only way to lose was if I quit. They were testing my ability to continue the mission, regardless of the circumstances.

The training was physically brutal and I started training harder than I ever had before. Twelve-mile runs, 16-mile road marches with rucksacks weighing 80 pounds, and intense weight training were incorporated into my daily life. While training for the road marches, the calluses on the bottoms of my feet blistered below the other calluses and the bottoms of my feet peeled off. During a 16-mile road march, I slipped and crashed hard. I hurt everywhere and struggled to get back up. I continued on and my knee started swelling so large my pants could barely contain the swelling. The medic asked why I was limping and I continued. If I had quit, I would have been gone. I pushed myself physically harder than I ever had before or since.

Just when I thought my fate was sealed, and I would be going away for extensive Army training, the ISP started working me through the hiring process. Over 3000 candidates had applied and only 50 were going to the academy. ISP was moving through their hiring process at an expedited rate and before I knew it, I had made it through the entire process and was only waiting on the final job offer. It was July and I knew the academy was starting in August. Time was running out so I was forced to gamble. I knew physically I could not continue with the Special Forces if I was hired by ISP and complete their 20-week academy. I also knew I was going to have to give my job at the group home a two weeks' notice.

It was now decision time. I still had not received word from ISP, but had to gamble. I transferred back to my MP unit and was informed I needed to leave immediately for annual training. I also gambled with my job and turned in my two weeks' notice. If I won the gamble, I was set up to start ISP on a good note. If I lost the gamble, I lost my job and my shot at Special Forces. It was now two weeks prior to the academy and still no offer from ISP. I was in the field training. I had no access to a phone or my mail. All I could do was focus on my Army training and put the rest in God's hands.

Activity

This chapter is rich in lessons. First, when you do not see a path forward, you need to blaze your own path. Sometimes, the quickest way to get from point (A) to point (B) is to go to points (C) and (D) first. Sometimes, God leads us on paths which do not make sense because there are lessons to be learned. With the group home, I learned a new level of compassion I had not experienced before. It was also humbling and reminded me of my blessings. I was reminded of this lesson recently when my boss and I went to lunch. He was having a very bad day and was in a bit of a snit. When he walked into the restaurant, his attitude changed. He observed a teenager with a disability. He told me seeing that teen reminded him of the blessings God had given him and the trials he was going through that day were trivial to the problems of that teen. He reacted to that teen with a new level of gratitude. That is one of the lessons I learned from the group home.

The next lesson is to pursue the path you are put on aggressively. When I was presented with the Special Forces opportunity, I had to throw myself into it totally to complete the rigors of the training. Doing the right thing in front of you and not planning the outcome leads to some remarkable progress. And, yes, "the right thing in front of you" is correct!

Another lesson is: the only time you actually lose is when you quit. You can fail a thousand times and not be a failure if you just do not quit. All it takes is that one victory to make you a winner. But you will never be a winner if you quit! Defying the odds has been big business for me. The real lesson is that sometimes you have to go through countless failings and find that one giant piece of success.

The final lesson is to go all in on your dreams. Gambling with such things as a job is scary. It affects our security, both financially and professionally. I am not talking reckless, flippant gambling. I am talking about thoughtful, deliberate gambling. The type of gambling where you put the result in God's hands because you have completed every possible task on your end.

Your activity is to recognize alternate paths you have been on before and write down the lessons or skills you learned from being sidetracked.

The next activity is to write down any time you failed something and just quit. Recognize quitting is the only thing which makes you a loser.

Next, write down three things for which you are grateful.

Finally, identify times when you placed your future in God's hands and trusted His outcome, not necessarily your anticipated outcome. Remember His will be done not my will be done.

Indiana State Police Headshot
(courtesy of Todd Griffee)

Chapter 5

Seize The Opportunity

The Army training was actually a lot of fun, but was very physically demanding. I worked my soldiers 20 hours a day because we had to pass our evaluations to be a deployable asset. On top of that, we were the Opposing Forces (OPFOR), who are the bad guys. We were doing double duty and I made it a point to provide the best training possible for my soldiers. I remember sitting in the rain on the landing zone when the battalion commander asked what my platoon was doing. I explained we were waiting on choppers to pick us up for several training missions. The battalion commander laughed at me and said he did not approve Army air support for me and he boasted no one would be flying in the rain anyway. As soon as he started smugly walking away, three Marine Corps Huey helicopters touched down, in the rain, and we quickly climbed aboard. The shocked look on the

"Old Man's" face was priceless. I thought to myself, don't tell me never! Needless to say, my OPFOR wreaked havoc on his battalion for the next week and dismantled his entire enterprise.

When there was a lull in the action, I snuck onto the civilized part of base and found a pay phone to call Michelle. It was a Wednesday evening and the ISP academy was starting Monday. Michelle said I received something from ISP earlier that day. It seemed like an eternity for her to open the envelope. Finally, she read I was accepted to the ISP Academy and was ordered to report first thing on Monday morning. I was stoked! I had just spent the past four years trying to get into law enforcement and my opportunity finally arrived!

The next few days were exhausting because we still needed to complete our evaluations and we passed them with flying colors. We packed all of our gear to head out of the field, but we were ordered to the battalion area of operations. The battalion had discovered I was the one who destroyed their unit in the exercise and it was payback time. The operations officer ordered me to have my platoon load his units gear onto their trucks. I verified with the Major that he wanted my people to load his people's gear onto their trucks. He replied that was a direct order, adding, "Do you have a problem with that, Lieutenant?" I replied, "No, Sir," saluted, did an about face and walked over to the platoon. I took off my BDU blouse and jumped in the back of the truck. I told my people I did not want to hear them complain, but advised them we would be loading their gear onto their trucks. We were loading the trucks when the Major yelled at me to get off of the truck and report to him. I reported to him and he asked what I was doing. I advised I was loading his gear on his trucks as ordered. He said, "You are an officer and you are doing manual labor. You are making us officers look bad." I replied, "Sir, I obeyed your order, even though I disagreed with it and I would not ask my people to do anything, I was unwilling to do myself." He blew his top, more than likely because he knew I was right. He dismissed me. When my platoon saw me leading by example, they respected and trusted me completely after that incident. We finally got back to the reserve center and were dismissed Sunday evening.

I was only able to get a couple hours of sleep before I had to leave for the ISP academy. The day started in the typical created chaos of the first day at an academy, lots of yelling and barking of orders. We had to report in a suit and tie, and remember, I just came out of the field with the Army so my hair was short. Very short! During the inspection, the lead instructor told me to get a haircut. I almost laughed out loud, but I had to make a decision. Do I want to be the student who is always hiding in the crowd, hoping nobody will notice them, or be the student who asks, how high, when they are told to jump? I went with the second answer. I had worked hard for four years to get here. Blending into the crowd was not the answer. I firmly answered, "Sir, yes, Sir." Later that night I had the barber shave my head. The instructors understood fully, during morning inspection, just how motivated I was to be there. It was a dangerous gamble because they all knew my name then, and any mistake I made would be put under a microscope. The training was very physical, with lots of physical training (PT), defensive tactics (fighting), Emergency Vehicle Operations Course (EVOC), and firearms instruction. It was made clear to us early on, if you did not like to shoot, drive fast, and fight, you were in the wrong place. I had a lot of fun learning those skills at the academy and they made the time go by quickly. We also had a lot of interesting scholastic training like criminal law and traffic law. Then we had crash investigation. I will just leave that there. Before I knew it the first 16 weeks were complete! Then it was like hitting a wall. All the fun classes were over and the last four weeks consisted of dry, required, filler classes. I think that was one of the slowest months of my life, but graduation day arrived and the sense of accomplishment I felt was hard to match.

The next step was the field training portion of the training. I was lucky my two primary field training officers (FTOs), were pretty high speed and were great teachers. Then there were the few days in between when I was placed with one of the "grumpy old men." Not fun.

When I was with my primary FTO, we completed a lot of traffic stops, made many DUI arrests, responded to domestic disturbances, and backed up county police on calls. It seemed like every night something exciting happened.

During the final days of training, I was with my secondary FTO, who was also aggressive. We received a call for a welfare check in a tiny farm town. The father of the people met us at the location and he was distraught. He advised us his granddaughter was writing prison inmates as part of their church ministry. The daughter ended up marrying one of the inmates when he was released from prison. The father said he felt like the convict did something to his children because the blinds were closed, the doors were locked, and the cars were in the garage. We made entry into the home and the first thing I observed was a man on the floor, who had been brutally beaten in the head with a hammer. We did not know if the subject was still in the house so we quietly continued to clear the house. In the downstairs bathroom, the wife was lying face down in the bathtub and her hands and feet were hog tied behind her back. She had been drowned. As I reached the top of the stairs, leading to the upstairs bedroom. I saw a body on the bed. It was one of the daughters, who had her pants pulled down and her hands and feet tied to the bed posts. She had been run through with a large kitchen knife. We immediately called for our crime scene technician and detectives, as we secured the scene. The father gave us the address to the subject's apartment, and as soon as we were able, we started on the manhunt for the subject. Just as we arrived at his apartment with backup from the local police, the post called us and ordered us to sit on the house because the prosecutor was going to wait until morning to get a warrant. The next day, we received a tip reporting a friend of the subject provided the subject with a car. I was stern with the friend who admitted giving his car to the subject, but pled ignorance to the fact his friend had just murdered three people. I advised the friend he was an accomplice to a murderer and could be imprisoned for it. I told the friend we missed the subject by 15 minutes today and made it clear we would not be late tomorrow. The friend swore up and down he had no contact with the subject. When I woke up the next morning, I saw the subject had driven to the neighboring state police district office. He woke up a pastor at a church who coordinated his surrender to ISP. The subject told our detectives he knew his in-laws hid cash in their cookie jar and when the father arrived, he was literally caught with his hand in the cookie jar so he killed the father. When the mother came home, he had to kill her, then his sister-in-law. This call was a real tragedy, but I felt fortunate to have assisted in his apprehension.

In no time, I completed my FTO, was issued my own vehicle, and was turned loose. Once again, I had to make a decision. Do I want to be the sort of Trooper who does the bare minimum to get by and hide in the crowd, or do I want to be a leader and be aggressive?

Activity

In this chapter, it had taken me over four years to receive this opportunity. I had to make a decision as to what I was going to do with the opportunity. Was I going to play it safe and do the bare minimum or was I going to push myself to achieve my fullest potential. I chose to push myself to be the best version of me I could be. God granted me this opportunity. It would not be right to put the light of His work under a basket, to shade it from everyone. He put me in the position to help people and I could not do that hiding in a donut shop.

Your activity is to envision attaining your opportunity and to write down a list of ideas, which would maximize the benefits of your accomplishment. Just like starting a new job. Plan out your first day, week, month, and year. What do you want to be recognized for? If it's a position of leadership, write down ideas describing your leadership style. This type of envisioning also helps provide positive reinforcement, which instills the concept that you will achieve your goal.

Chapter 6

Never Routine

I am sure you guessed that I was going to be a go getter. God put me in this career for a reason. Now it was my chance to get to work. I was aggressive but fair with traffic enforcement. I wrote a lot of warnings and tried to view every contact I had with the general public as an opportunity to represent ISP in a positive light. But I also got a lot of drunks off the road. On New Year's Eve one year, I arrested a drunk driver within 15 minutes of going on shift. After I completed the hours of paperwork at the jail, I went back on patrol. Within 10 minutes, a truck exiting the toll road ran me off the road. Back to the jail for more paperwork. I made it out of the jail with just enough time to respond to two bar fights before heading home. I also used traffic patrol to build criminal cases and got a lot of guns, drugs, and wanted people off the street. I also responded to criminal investigations; it was the extensive criminal investigation experience I received at ISP which would serve me so well later in my career.

We also assisted local police agencies with calls, especially county police, who were always out- numbered. I became great friends with a lot of county police because of that close working relationship. I prided myself in being a policeman's policeman. One evening on my scanner I overheard one of my friends who was working in the north patrol zone, get dispatched to a burglary complaint. When he arrived at the subject's residence, a large group of people rushed out of the house and started moving toward my friend, making threats. He got on the radio and yelled for backup. The other north car was busy on another call and the dispatcher accidentally called my friend to back himself up. I figured out the dilemma so I put the hammer down, screamed into the subject's yard, jumped out of my car, racked my 12-gauge shotgun, and told everyone to get back on the porch. Later, my friend thanked me and said that was the best noises he heard, when he was in trouble... a roaring engine, squealing tires, and the deafening rack of that shotgun.

I also got to work special events like county fairs, the Indianapolis 500™, the Brickyard 400™, and of course, Notre Dame Football games. I really enjoyed those games and loved meeting all the cool people involved. Then there where the other special details. I was "voluntold" to be on the Tactical Intervention Platoon (TIP) Squad. We worked all sorts of controversial rallies and rotated into crime suppression patrols in Gary, IN, which was then the murder capital of the world, per capita. That was like working in the Wild West, and we got into some crazy pursuits with murder suspects. I recall one of the "grumpy old troopers" sitting in a donut shop. When I walked in, he loudly bragged about never having to pull out his pistol in 20 years. I responded that maybe he should go to work in Gary, because there, pulling out your pistol was called "hospitality."

Police work is hardly routine and this came to light when a detective from a local agency in a county south of my patrol zone responded to a house to interview a subject's wife. It was going to be a quick interview so he left his pistol and radio in his car and went up to the house to ask a couple of quick questions. During that short time, the subject showed up and surprised him. The subject shot and killed the detective, his own wife, and his own toddler son. The subject fled the scene and evaded the manhunt. When I started to respond, my Sergeant told me I worked the last homicide so I needed to stay behind and respond to all of the county calls because the county sent their entire patrol division to assist with the manhunt. It was not pleasant doing vehicle inspections and "cat in the tree" types of responses when everyone else was doing something dangerous. The following day, the subject was still at large and I had a feeling something was going to break free so I stayed near the border within the county where the murders happened. We had detectives and technicians processing the scene when I heard the locals kick up a pursuit. The post attempted to reach our people on scene but they did not respond. When I attempted to inform the post, I was en route, they told me to keep quiet because they were on radio silence. I hit my lights and siren and went anyway. Normally when you are running lights and siren, people will not get out of your way. I actually did an experiment once where I ran to an emergency with lights and siren and observed countless people obstructing my path. The next emergency, I ran silent with no lights. I just turned on my radar. Nobody got in my way, when they were worried about getting a ticket. In this case, everyone moved out of the way, like Moses parting the

Red Sea. The shooting had stopped seconds before I arrived on scene. There were bullet holes all over the police car, the gas station, and the truck the subject stole the night before. It looked like a gangster movie scene and there were bullet casings everywhere. It is a miracle no bystanders were hit. I ran to the subject's truck and it looked like somebody spilled a five gallon bucket of blood everywhere; he was gurgling. Once he was secured, the medics loaded him onto a helicopter to transport him to a hospital. We taped off the entire block, and started processing the crime scene, when the loud speaker on the fire truck announced the subject died on the way to the hospital. Thousands of townspeople had gathered around the crime scene and when they heard the announcement, they cheered like some Medieval mob witnessing an execution. It was a very primal experience to witness.

Another night, the post ordered me to meet with three other troopers to serve a murder warrant the next county over. The subject thought it would be cool to use a potato as a silencer on his revolver and shot a woman in the head. We received a tip he was hanging out in a trailer by a lake. One veteran trooper took a rookie with him and I took the other rookie. It was dark and raining when we started down this dirt road with our headlights off for surprise. The trooper in front of me had trouble seeing and turned on his headlights. When he did that, I saw this muscular bare-chested guy with a giant stick duck down behind a pickup truck. I yelled at the rookie to get on the radio and tell the car in front I had the guy. I ran over to the pickup and once again racked that shotgun and told the subject to get on the ground. He dropped the stick and assumed a prone handcuffing position, while the troopers from the lead car cuffed him. We then hit the trailer and verified we had the correct person on the warrant. It was him. We drove back to our staging area so everyone could pick up their vehicle. In that process, one trooper said he wanted his cuffs back before they took the subject to jail. Rather than put a new set on him, then remove the old cuffs, they let him out of the cuffs and told him to put his hands on his head. Then they started discussing different handcuffing techniques. I was already back in my car when this was going on. I noticed the subject started looking around and flexing his muscles. He was going to fight. I ran over there and nudged his head with my shotgun and told him not to move. He was startled, but the other troopers quickly cuffed him. I asked the subject, "What were you doing, standing behind that truck, with no shirt, in the rain, with that giant stick?" He replied it was not a stick; it was a martial arts staff. The hairs on the back of my neck went up because those troopers came really close to something bad happening. Criminals are kind of like dogs in the sense that they smell fear. When a dog senses you are scared, it will attack. That is how criminals react to fear, as well.

Months later, my lieutenant, asked me to conduct traffic patrols in a little town which had a speeding problem. I would head there a couple times a week to make my presence known and the townspeople appreciated the extra service. One night, I was on a traffic stop in this town when the dispatcher informed me of a shooting at a gas station on the south side of that town. I ran back up to the car I had stopped, gave them their license back, and told them to evacuate the area. I shut off all of my lights, and rolled around the corner to the gas station, where I saw a guy in a black ski mask holding a sawed off shotgun. I did not even have time to grab my shotgun. I drew my pistol and ordered the subject to drop the gun. He refused. I kept yelling at him. I was finally able to order the guy to his knees, while he was facing away from me. I ordered him a final time to drop the gun, when he started turning around with it. We carried Beretta pistols which had a long trigger pull on the first shot, and short ones following the original shot. I went into tunnel vision, focused on my front sight, and started squeezing that long trigger pull. The hammer was moving rearward, when the subject dropped the gun. It seemed like an eternity, but was probably less than a split second. I ordered the subject to stand up and walk backward towards my voice. He started moving rearward, but he put his hand in his pocket and turned around. I had moved my position so he would not know exactly where I was. When he turned around my adrenaline dumped. I threw him on the ground and the knife in his pocket and shotgun shells flew out of his pockets. I cuffed him and put him in the car before the first backup car arrived. The post had been calling me and I was a little too busy to answer so they sent the cavalry. The first on the scene was one of our detectives, who responded from home; the second cars to arrive were the two county cars from the north zone. They crossed an entire county to back me up. The subject was a convicted felon and I charged him with many more. Unbeknownst to me, the complainant who had called in the shots fired was hiding in a phone booth and saw the whole thing. He told the detective I did an amazing job because I was able to arrest the guy without shooting him.

Activity

In police training, they engrain in your very psyche that there is nothing routine about anything in police work. You hear the news regularly that a police officer was killed during a routine traffic stop or during a routine response to a domestic disturbance. The minute a police officer becomes complacent and treats things as routine is the minute he places himself in great peril. The same attitude can be used in any career. It is important to be alert and have your head in the game. So often people start just going through the motions and become complacent. This leads to lots of missed opportunities/promotions, or reading the writing on the wall when something bad is coming. Sometimes we are in jobs we do not like, but it is important to build the habit of doing your best to do good work and learn lessons you can utilize later in life.

Your activity is to write down things you can improve in your current position that you can utilize later. Remember this builds the habit of constantly striving to succeed and knowing your surroundings. Being alert and conscientious can take you far in life!

Chapter 7

Sacrifices

I was working crazy overtime and was busy in the Army Reserves. There were days when I would get home from work, shower, change into my Army uniform, and drill for a weekend with no sleep. On the relationship side of things, Michelle suffered a miscarriage, which was heart-breaking. We were so looking forward to this child. We were going to name him Connor. I supported her emotionally as best as possible, but it became harder and harder. I was unable to provide her with the support she needed. After several months, I mistakenly told her she needed to find a way to get over the loss. I had good intentions, but it did not matter how nicely I tried to convey my support. Michelle would resent me for years after that incident. We started fighting more, and I started drinking more. It was a vicious circle.

We managed to finally start moving forward, when great news arrived. She was pregnant again. We were thrilled. When she was overdue, I was working the next county over. I had a "go bag" for her to take to the hospital once she was ready. One night, the post called and told me to call my wife because it was an emergency. I called and she said, "You better hurry! It is time!" I put that cruiser at full speed and made record time getting home (it was late at night and there was no traffic on the road). I told myself, be cool, I am trained for this sort of thing. I calmly placed a towel on the front seat of my patrol car, loaded her luggage, and sat her in front. I slowly pulled out of the parking lot when she screamed her water just broke. The calm went right out the window. I hit the lights and siren and put my racing skills to task. I called the post and they called the hospital to alert them of my arrival. A county police friend of mine was working part time at the hospital and was waiting at the entrance with a wheel chair. I came flying up, sliding the car sideways into the entrance drive. My friend quickly loaded up Michelle and rushed her inside. I parked the car and ran in. The doctor threw me a mask and gown and said, "Hurry. We need to rush to surgery because the umbilical cord is wrapped around the baby's neck. He is suffocating." I threw on the gown, and they instantly put Michelle under. They made the incision and lifted out my son. He made it into this world unharmed. Thank God! I remind him often his life depended on my driving prowess.

My son was born! I was so scared we would not have enough money while Michelle stayed home after giving birth so I got a part time job and worked before going on duty every day. The baby was a fun kid and everyone adored him, but Michelle and I started arguing again. I was exhausted with working all the time, and Michelle was upset I was not home more. This lead to more arguing and I responded with more drinking. One day, it was one argument too many, and Michelle told me she wanted a divorce, and moved back to Florida. I was sick to my stomach. My little buddy would not be around. I was heartbroken and sick. The sense of failure I felt was devastating. I was embarrassed to tell my family I was getting divorced. I felt low. Somehow I threw myself into my work and into the bottle to manage.

To complicate things, I had reapplied to the DEA and was moving through their process. I figured that without my family I would be free to relocate. Then Michelle and I started talking and decided to reconcile. I flew down to Florida to visit them and it was wonderful. I rented a moving truck and moved them back to Indiana. My son rode in the U-Haul with me. For a little one year old, he kept me great company. Soon afterward my daughter arrived but without the high drama of my son's arrival. She was such a happy baby; she smiled at me the first time I held her. It was an awesome feeling to have my family back. Then I received my conditional hire from DEA. They wanted to send me to New York City on a GS-5 pay for my first assignment. I would have been able to handle the assignment as a single guy, but not likely for a family. Michelle flat out objected! She wanted no part of New York, DEA, or letting me go to New York and travel home every month to visit.

Now came decision time. From 10 years old, all I wanted to be was a federal agent. Now the opportunity was handed to me. I could not just give up my dream, but I also could not give up my family, which I just got back. I considered all aspects, and was very happy with ISP, so I sacrificed my career for my family. On one hand I am very grateful for being able to spend time with my children when they were young. On the other hand, I started to become resentful of losing my dream. This would later manifest into my drinking career.

Activity

In life there are responsibilities which can get in the way of our dreams. Family and other obligations can be roadblocks to achieving them. This can be clearly seen with professional women. How many successful women have children, decide to put their family as a priority, and miss their dream? They can be distracted with the responsibilities of being a parent, but when the empty nest hits, is there an opportunity to chase their dream again? Only you can make what is the best decision for you.

Your activity is to write down responsibilities which interfere(d) with your dreams. Write down the pros and cons of your decision and ways to cope with your decision so you can prevent the resentment creeping up and manifesting itself with destructive behavior. Also, identify alternate avenues to attaining your goal.

Chapter 8

Hero to Zero

After the decision not to go to DEA, the dust settled and we were able to get our first home. It was a real fixer upper, but it was in a nice neighborhood. Family and friends helped us gut the house and remodel it. We made it a home and it was a fantastic feeling having my family together. Life was good.

Remember when I told you one of the great perks of being with ISP was working the Notre Dame home football games? South Bend during game weekends is full of excitement, with people from around the country joining the celebration. This hype is what I grew up in, and was one of the key factors which drove me to attend Notre Dame. Indeed, Notre Dame is a very special place. On game day weekends, I would work an earlier shift so I would be off by 8:30 PM, in order to work a long day on Saturday. One October game day weekend, I got off work and went to a local Notre Dame bar to see some friends, some of whom came in from out of town. It was a fun night and it was good to catch up with old classmates I had not seen since graduation. I was friends with the owners and all the off duty police who worked security. When I was growing up, my father owned a tavern not far from there so I knew a lot of people in the bar business.

Closing time came and my friends and I were getting ready to leave, when someone ran inside and screamed for help. As an Indiana State Trooper, you are on duty 24-hours a day and are obligated to take action. I ran outside and saw two males violently beating a student on the ground with very large flashlights. This was not a silly bar fight, this was a potentially deadly situation. I knew I had been drinking so I did not want to just jump in the melee, but I was obligated to do something. I yelled for the security to call the local police. I noted the subjects' vehicle engine was running and it was parked on the road. I decided to run to the vehicle and remove the keys so the subjects could not escape. As I reached my hand through the steering wheel to remove the keys, I was smashed in the head with one of those heavy flashlights. I saw a flash and my ears went numb. I had taken some nasty blows to the head in the Army and this was really the last thing I needed. Time became distorted and it took me an eternity to recognize what was going on. The subjects jumped back into the truck and were attempting to flee. I kept screaming, "State Police, Stop, State Police, Stop!" They continued their deadly assault. By now blood was running down my face and into my eyes. I tried with all my might to pull the driver from the vehicle. I was fighting for my life. When they say people who face deadly situations see their life pass in front of their eyes, they are correct. I saw the faces of my family and my training kicked in. If I wanted to see my family again, I was going to have to stay in the fight to win. I pulled out my pistol and tried to shoot the driver, but he slammed the truck in gear and started to take off. All I saw were faces of innocent bystanders on the other side of the truck so I did not have a clear shot. The driver swerved hard to the left, striking me with the side of the truck. This removed the bystanders from being in the way so I let it rip. Between the tunnel vision, the blood in my eyes, and my hearing being absent, I thought my pistol jammed because I never heard it go off. The subjects fled. It ended up that I fired so fast, witnesses only heard two shots, when I actually fired six. I hit the subjects' truck four times and somehow managed to miss the occupants. I immediately called the post and requested a supervisor. I was bleeding profusely and both thumbs were in extreme pain from getting hit repeatedly with the flashlights as I attempted to defend myself. My head was on fire, ringing, and I did not know if I just wanted to pass out or throw up. I did not want to go to the hospital with the ambulance because I needed to turn my pistol over to a supervisor or detective.

A detective showed up shortly, followed by the first sergeant and he transported me to the hospital. I asked for a breathalyzer because that was the state standard for toxicology. I had drunk ten beers, but it was over quite a long time. I wanted to have it on record I was not intoxicated. He took me to the hospital and had them do a blood draw, which at the time was not the state standard. The blood serum results came back as .07% BAC (which converts to .04% BAC by breath) and the legal limit at the time was .10 BAC so I was under. The hospital treated me and stitched me up. I looked like a raccoon with both eyes blackened. The department attorney (very nice man and one of our instructors at the academy) drove up and interviewed me at the hospital. Then I was transported to Notre Dame Police Department to be interviewed by a state police detective. The interview was recorded and I was forthright with my answers. They drilled it into our heads at the academy that it was okay to make mistakes and the department would stand behind you as long as you were honest and cooperative. I took that as gospel, cooperated, and was honest. The detective took me home around 11:00 AM. I was absolutely drained and exhausted so I crashed.

The next thing I knew, the news media got hold of the story and made me out to be the bad guy because the public affairs officer did not release factual information to the news media. I called him, asked what he was doing, and told him what he gave the media was not what happened. He replied he could not fix it because it would look like a cover-up. It was embarrassing because I was one of the leading troopers in my district and prided myself on doing great work. Then, my grandfather said he saw the news and they described me as a disgrace to the uniform. That was heartbreaking. Then the area captain tried to get me suspended, when the superintendent stepped in and said I was to report back to duty as soon as I was medically cleared. My immediate chain of command was very supportive, along with the detectives who worked the case and had located the subjects at their cousin's house because he was a local police officer. The case was submitted to the prosecutor's office for review, with me listed as the victim for a battery on a police officer case. I reported back to work on Monday with two black eyes and two fractured thumbs. I still felt like I'd been hit by a truck, but I wanted everyone to know I was not suspended. I continued aggressively doing my job and actually had the best evaluation I ever received at ISP based on my traffic enforcement and criminal investigation efforts.

Life started to get back to normal as I healed and the news media died down. Then in February of the next year, my sergeant (who was a great guy I loved working for) called me at home on a Friday morning. He told me to unload all of my guns and have them on the kitchen table. He told me to also have the keys to my state police car and credentials on the table. He used to prank me all the time so I thought he was joking. He said, sadly, he was not. He said the prosecutor filed for a warrant for two felonies against me. He was coming to take me to jail and the bond was high. I did as he asked and while I waited I called my dad who, thankfully, was able to help with the bond money and said he would meet me at the jail. I then called my county buddy and told him. He was shocked and recommended an attorney named Charlie who was the best in town. There was an attorney friend (or brother-in-law) of the prosecutor who was known for getting good plea deals for the right amount of money, but my friend said I needed an attorney who could beat the prosecutor because I did not do anything wrong. I called Charlie's office and he told me to come to his office as soon as I bonded out of jail. As soon as I hung up, my supervisor showed up, collected my items, and had another trooper with him, who would be driving my state police car. My own state police car followed me to jail. How messed up is that? When I arrived at the jail, I was met by my father and the sheriff who was a longtime family friend. The sheriff explained he got into an argument with the prosecutor because the prosecutor asked for a high bond and wanted me arrested on Friday so I would have to sit in jail all weekend or longer if I could not bond out. The warrant actually came down on Wednesday, so I literally arrested someone on a warrant when I also had an active warrant out on me. That is some shady stuff right there. The sheriff said he told the prosecutor he would not house a state trooper in his jail. The sheriff had me quickly booked, printed, and had my mug photo completed. He then took us out a tunnel so I would avoid the news media waiting outside.

The next stop was Charlie's office. He grilled me for an hour and concluded with his decision that he would represent me. I was thankful because he was very thorough and well respected. On Monday, I was back in court for my arraignment. The sheriff went with me to the hearing and Charlie entered a not guilty plea for me. My trial was set for August. That six months seemed like an eternity.

My supervisor had advised me that I was on administrative duty and I was to report to the Toll Road District on Tuesday. They would not even let me go to my home post. I reported and was tasked with completing the data entry of all of the tickets written by the district. The secretary was snarky and curt. She was always badgering me to work faster. I was trying to be a good scout and do my admin time because I was innocent until proven guilty. I was confident I would be back on the road soon. The other troopers avoided me like I had the plague, except for one, who had also been involved in a shooting. He was a great support and the only thing even closely resembling counseling for the ordeal I went through. Now the department has mandatory counseling services. My situation was also complicated by the fact we received a new superintendent who ordered the termination of all troopers who had Internal Investigations pulled on them. This superintendent went on to be the director of a federal agency and was terminated. That brought me some satisfaction later in life. Meanwhile, Charlie spoke with my lieutenant and recommended it would be better for me to resign than to be fired, in case I wanted to return to law enforcement. It was a dark day when I resigned. I wanted to vomit, thinking about the four years I spent getting to ISP and the four years I spent excelling at ISP. Now, in a split second, it was over.

Activity

In this chapter I was the victim of a very violent crime. That in itself is a traumatic ordeal which is hard for people to overcome. Then I lost my reputation. I spent years building a professional presence and was now being chased by the news media like I was one of the "Ten Most Wanted." The state police had taken all my firearms, and the news media reported my address. I had arrested hundreds of people who now knew where I lived and that my authority to arrest was suspended. I was not even able to protect myself because you cannot purchase a firearm while you are charged with a felony. I lost my career, which had been a dream of mine since I was ten years old. But I also left a job which was providing for my family and our new house. Honestly, this was very difficult to write because it infuriates me how the victim becomes the subject and a misquote from public affairs destroyed my reputation; how a prosecutor with an agenda can destroy my livelihood and an agency I loved who did not lift a finger to support me. I was feeling hopeless. Looking back, the thing which kept me sane was the love and support of my family, friends, and extended family. Without that support system, I would never have made it. Despite things getting worse and worse, God gave me the strength and guidance not to give up. This is clearly an example of when life hits you so hard, you have no idea how you are going to get back up. All the wind is knocked out of you.

Your activity for this chapter is to identify life changing events which happened to you. In the next category, write down how it affected you. Was it a save face issue, was it a sex issue, or was it a financial issue? Something else? It is not only important to identify the what, but the how. The next thing is to write down all the members of your support system. Who can you count on when the chips are down? Writing down this material helps you process the ordeal and provide insight and preparation in case you run into another ordeal. Remember, I am sharing these things so you can know you are not alone in your suffering and to provide hope that God can and will take care of you.

Chapter 9

Judged by 12

There I was, frantically trying to find work to support my family. After being character assassinated by the news media, I was pretty much a hot potato. The sheriff knew my work ethic and said he would gladly hire me, but he could not hire me with a felony conviction. He did say he would hire me with a misdemeanor conviction. I swallowed my pride for my family and asked Charlie to ask for a misdemeanor plea deal so I could take care of my family. That decision was humiliating because I did not do anything wrong and was the victim of a violent crime, but I put my family first. My pride was not going to keep a roof over my family's head or food in their bellies. Charlie returned from a meeting with the prosecutor who said I was not in line for misdemeanor treatment. Now what?

I saw an ad in the newspaper for a foreman in a plastics factory and was hired. I did my best learning a new trade because I might be stuck in it for a while. I was up front with them and advised them I had a trial in August. They said the time off would be no problem because I was salary and I would be working over 40 hours and that would compensate for the missed days. It did not pay as well as ISP, and I was so far behind in bills from being unemployed, I was forced into bankruptcy.

It seemed like an eternity for August to arrive. I was anxious to get my life and reputation back. About a week before my trial, a friend of mine who was a local police officer was murdered in the line of duty. Absolutely heartbreaking! I attended his funeral and it was the biggest funeral I had ever seen. It really bothered me seeing hundreds of other police officers when I'd had that privilege stripped from me. I was more than ready to get out of limbo and get the trial rolling. When we appeared in court to make the final arrangements for the trial, the prosecutor asked to move the court date because another defendant wanted a speedy trial. Actually, the other defendant's attorney requested a continuance and the judge denied it. So that trial was scheduled during my trial, which moved my trial to the following January. That was emotionally catastrophic. Six more months in purgatory. That made me despise my job at the plastics factory even more. It did not help when my boss' boss would screw with me. He was always belittling, and when they needed someone to run a shift on Saturday, he would order me to do it, rather than the hourly-waged foreman who was junior to me. They were getting free work out of me and taking advantage of the situation.

A week before the new trial, the prosecutor asked Charlie if I wanted to accept a misdemeanor plea bargain. I told Charlie exactly where he could tell the prosecutor to stick that plea bargain. When it was convenient for me to take a plea bargain to take care of my family and avoid bankruptcy, they would not hear it. Now they wanted it. I did not do anything wrong. If I were convicted, there was a two year mandatory prison sentence. I told Charlie I would rather go to prison than to admit I was wrong. Charlie agreed and advised me I had burned threw my retainer. He said he knew I did not have the money, but said he believed in me and was doing the rest of the case pro bono. I nearly cried out of gratitude. It was not just the money (that was a huge deal), it was having someone who would fight for me.

I am sure you have heard the expression, it is better to be judged by twelve, than carried by six, meaning it is better to leave your fate to twelve jurors as opposed to being carried by six pall bearers. Honestly, at this point, I thought it would have been better to be carried by six because this "judged by twelve" had already stolen a year out of my life and bankrupted me.

The week of the trial finally arrived and I was informed by my boss at the plastics factory that I would have to go in to work those days. I explained what I was promised when I started, but they would not budge. All those Saturdays I worked meant nothing. I was expected to go in, fire up all of the machines, and set up all the crews, then I could leave for trial. Every morning I went in, did my work, ran home, showered, put on a suit, and was nearly late for trial every day. Nothing like adding more stress to the equation.

Tuesday began with jury selection and opening statements. On Wednesday and Thursday, the prosecution started his case with nearly 20 witnesses. Most of the witnesses were actually great witnesses for me because I was the original victim in the case. The exception was the donut eating, self-righteous trooper I mentioned earlier, in Chapter 6, but he did not see anything and his testimony was irrelevant. Charlie did a fantastic job cross examining the witnesses. Then the prosecutor called the two original subjects to the stand, one at a time. Previously, Charlie took sworn depositions from the two of them and they lied their pants off. When I asked Charlie about it, he said do not worry. As soon as he started cross examining them, I knew why. He kept using their depositions to demonstrate they perjured themselves. They admitted to the perjury, to using deadly force while beating two students who they thought threw a bottle at their truck, and to hearing me identifying myself as state police. They admitted to using deadly force by hitting me in the head and admitted to attacking me to get away and avoid apprehension. Soon, everyone was curious why I was charged and they were not. The prosecution ended by playing my tape recorded statement I made to the ISP detective when I was first released from the hospital. I was actually a witness for the prosecution.

Friday morning was a gut check. It was our turn and I was the only witness for the defense. If I screwed up, I was going to prison. Plain and simple. I got on the stand and Charlie did a fantastic job with his questions. Then the prosecutor started in and his sole aim was to anger and provoke me. He wanted the jury to see me angry. With God's help, I was able to keep my cool. The cooler I was, the more vicious his attacks became. I had to trust Charlie would pick up the pieces and set the jury straight during re-examination. Charlie did just that. That was it. If we lost it would not be because I choked.

Then the prosecutor made his closing remarks and Charlie made his closing remarks and sounded like an attorney you would see on TV. He was amazing. Finally the prosecutor made the final remarks. The prosecutor picked up my pistol (still in the evidence packaging) and started slamming it on the jury rail. He started screaming, "Send a message, no more police brutality!" He kept repeating those words and slamming my pistol. Charlie jumped up and objected faster than a vampire startled out of its coffin. The Judge agreed and let Charlie make the closing statements. Charlie told the jury the prosecutor's actions were the most unprofessional, unethical, and improper thing he had ever seen in his long history of practicing law. He explained to the jury that their duty was to determine if I violated the letter of the law, not to send a message. He told the jury, "This State Trooper risked his life to help others," and then asked if they were going to throw my life away for doing it.

The Judge provided the jury with their final instructions and sent them to deliberate. Now the waiting began.

Activity

This chapter covers several types of people you will encounter during life. During this trial I had a lot of family and friends show up to support me. That meant the world. Then there was Charlie, who was like an angel from heaven saving the day. There was the witnesses who had the courage to tell the truth. There was the opportunist witness, whose sole aim was to discredit me. There were the subjects, who admitted actually committing the crimes and lying about it. There were the jurors, who were trying to make sense of a case where the victim is charged, but not the subject. Finally there was the prosecutor, who had an agenda because an election was coming soon.

For this activity, write down the names of those people in your life and place them into similar groups I discussed above. Sort out who God has sent into your life and who the devil has sent to tempt or hurt you. This exercise should help you identify red flags in your relationships so you know who you can trust and who you should avoid. Also write down times when you were tested to the max. I was the only witness for the defense. If I screwed up, I was going to prison. Identify how you got through that test and that is how and where you will see the hand of God working in your life.

Chapter 10

Vindication

Michelle and I left the courthouse because it was Friday and we had bills to pay. It is funny, the world does not stop just because you are dealing with a major life changing event. Sometimes that is a hard pill to swallow. I literally felt the weight of the world on my shoulders and people were just going about their routines as if it was a normal day. I really did not expect a decision to be made by the jury soon; I expected it by the end of the day or Monday, so the sheriff gave me a pager (cell phones were a rarity and super expensive at this time) in case a decision came down. It was less than an hour later when the sheriff paged me to return to the courthouse. The suspense was unbearable and I started to feel my body shake. I have been in deadly, dangerous situations before, but my anxiety was not nearly as high as when I drove back to court.

Michelle and I made it back to the courthouse and court resumed. The jury handed the decision to bailiff, who handed it to the judge. The judge read it to himself and looked around. It was as if time stood still. He started reading it aloud and said, "In the case of the State of Indiana versus Todd... Guilty." There were gasps around court room. I felt like I was punched in the stomach and started to double over in pain. The Judge quickly corrected himself and said, "In the case of the State of Indiana versus Todd J Griffee, the jury finds the defendant NOT GUILTY on both counts!" There were cheers all over the courtroom and lots of handshakes, thank yous, and hugs. A year and a half of hell was over! In Indiana, an acquittal by jury trial is a total exoneration of any wrongdoing. I got my reputation back and could get back to the field I missed so badly. Mum saw a reporter as we exited the court. I thought she was going to throw him down the stairs. She told him the media dragged my name through the mud and did not have all the facts. She kept going on about how damaging and irresponsible they were. She finally told him they better set the record straight. We went back to my parents' and had a huge celebration!

The next morning there was a tiny blip on the news stating I was acquitted and a smidgen of an article in the paper. Those people hounded me, destroyed my name, and when it was discovered I was not the bum they portrayed me to be, they did the bare minimum to set the record straight. Disgusting.

I spoke with the bailiff who worked this trial and he said the jury selected a jury foreman and had lunch. They asked the judge for clarification about state troopers being on duty 24-hours a day. He said they did not even deliberate 20 minutes and were puzzled how this even came to trial. One and a half years lost out of my life decided in minutes.

The sheriff said he wanted the dust to settle before hiring me because it was an election year. Monday morning I returned to the plastics factory and continued the drudgery. After a couple of weeks I was on one of my machines helping two of the operators with an issue so they could make bonus, when my boss' boss arrived. He started berating and belittling me in front of my crew and really gave me a dressing down. It was over nothing. There were no safety or production issues; this was just an egotistical show of force. I had put up with this man's attitude for over a year and the only reason I did was because I had to provide for my family. By this point I'd had enough and my state trooper/army officer self returned. I looked down at him squarely in the eye and politely asked him who in the bloody hell did he think he was talking to. I told him I did not back down from a prosecutor who tried to send me to prison, so why would I tolerate his behavior? I told him to get off my machine before my operators lost their bonus. He complied and locked himself in his office. My crew had a new respect for me after that incident. Weeks later, it was bonus time. My production numbers were pretty good and I worked all those Saturdays and during my trial week. I thought that would be good for something. I was informed by my boss (who actually was a really great guy), I would not be receiving a bonus. I was the only foreman to not receive a bonus. That was the last straw. I turned in my keys at the end of the shift and walked out. That was the only time I never gave a two weeks' notice. If the plastics factory did not care enough about me to give me a bonus, then I would return the favor in kind. I ran into my boss years later and he told me his boss was fired for getting caught having an affair with the shipping manager. I have to admit that was good news.

Luckily, a security company picked me up right away and I worked a ton of hours. Definitely light years better than the factory. Now I was just biding my time to get into the county police. The phone rang and it was the sheriff.

Activity

My dad told me years after the trial that I had more guts than anyone else he had ever met. He said he would have taken the plea deal. He told me I was right and he knew I knew I was right, and I was willing to risk it all to save my name. That was the biggest compliment that man had ever given me and he gave me a lot. I believe that is the first time he truly recognized me as a man.

There are times in life when you have to eat humble pie, and there are times you need to defend your honor and integrity. The important thing is knowing when to utilize which. This reminds me of the Serenity Prayer: "God, grant me serenity to accept the things I cannot change, the courage to change the things I can, and the wisdom to know the difference."

Your activity is to write down circumstances you had to endure and identify why. Next write down circumstances where you stood up for yourself and document why that situation was different. You will be able to see a pattern which you can learn from to help with the wisdom part of the exercise. So much of life is learning how to react to an obstacle, learn from it, and grow to improve your reaction to the next obstacle.

Todd Griffee

Chapter 11

Back in the Saddle

Like the old adage, if you get thrown off your horse, get right back in the saddle, and that is exactly what I did. The sheriff called and told me to go to the uniform shop to pick up my uniforms because I was to report for duty first thing Monday morning.

I arrived on Monday and was greeted with a warm welcome because I had formed a lot of friendships within this agency, during my time as a trooper. It was a breath of fresh air to be actually wanted instead of being tolerated. The sheriff said the game plan was for me to run the inmate commissary department until after the election. Then I would be promoted to road patrol. I was just glad to be there. The commissary program sold items like snacks, underwear, and writing utensils to the inmates. Every week they would send in an order and their account would be charged and I would deliver it. The prices and the selection was sparse. The profit from this program went to items needed for the training department so as not to burden the taxpayer. I saw this as an opportunity to make the department more money. I increased the selection to promote sales, and adjusted the pricing to maximize profits without ripping off the inmates. I would price the items at a local store carrying the same items and bump down the price a bit. This really boosted our profit. The commissary program also handled the accounts for pay phone revenue. That was a huge money maker. When an inmate was booked into the jail, the jail would take their cash and deposit it into the inmate trust fund. When the inmate was released, they would receive a check from that account. Every morning I would make the deposit for the previous day. I would be waiting at the bank doors when they opened with deposits sometimes over $50k.

Things at home started to improve again and Michelle gave birth to our youngest daughter. She was an easy baby during delivery and you could just see that special sparkle in her eyes. My mother was the youngest child and felt that bond with her. It used to make the older kids so mad because she would get away with things that would have got the other two kids in trouble. They would always tattle on her to me saying grandma was spoiling her.

I also decided to come out of retirement and started fencing again. I trained with the Notre Dame team and a local club. My right side had gotten pretty beat up in the Army, and my shoulder did not have the strength to hold the epee. I switched to being a lefty. I shot left handed, threw left handed, and ate left handed so the transition was easy. It took about a month of foot work drills to get my feet in synch. Once I got the rust off, I became very competitive and actually won a big local tournament. When I competed in national events I would always see fencers wearing Army, Navy, or Air Force warm ups. The military was sponsoring them to compete, so I contacted the Army and started the process of having the Army sponsor me to compete nationally.

Activity

After the black cloud of the trial dissipated, my life started to mend itself back to a positive state. I found myself able to plan new goals and seek new adventures. Hope was in the air. Even though life can be brutal, it can also be healing and hopeful.

Your activity is to focus on the positive things in your life and make a gratitude list. So much of life is trouble-shooting problems that we forget to look at the beautiful, rewarding aspects of life. God created this beautiful world and sometimes it is important to just pause and smell the roses.

Chapter 12

Midnights in the Jail

Election time rolled around and I just knew the sheriff was going to win his re-election. He did not. I was crushed. Here I made it back into the saddle and my future was once again uncertain. The new sheriff arrived and I submitted my resume, outlining my traffic enforcement and criminal investigation experience. The new sheriff came to my office and told me I was to report to midnights in the jail. What a slap in the face. The good thing was I got to work with all of my friends because we all got sent to midnights in the jail. My first night, the local police brought in an inmate they had beat up pretty badly in the street. He was in a restraining chair and was a mess. I kept him up all night chatting with him because he had a head injury. The last thing I needed was for him to die in the jail my first night. The new chief made it clear I was not going to be promoted. There was an incident where a murder suspect tried to shank an officer and started fighting with two officers. I immediately jumped in and pepper sprayed the suspect so we could cuff him. I was the hearing officer and charged the inmate with 10 days in solitary confinement, per our policy. I was called into the warden's office and asked why I used so much force to restrain the inmate and why I sentenced him to 10 days in the hole. My boss and I explained I followed department policy and procedure. I knew the real story; they were just looking for ways to make life miserable for anyone who had backed the previous sheriff.

My boss's wife owned a Notre Dame bar in town and I grew up in the bar business. My future with county was short-lived so I started planning. I worked all night and spent all day researching and gathering information for my next adventure. I was going to open an authentic British pub. If I kept the location of the pub in an unincorporated area of the county, I could generate a new liquor license relatively cheap. But if it was in the city, it could be hundreds of thousands of dollars. I did not have money like that. My realtor had a connection at a local bank and set up a meeting with him in an attempt to get a business loan. He said he would have to clear it with the board of directors. Guess who was the on the board of directors? That is correct – the prosecutor. I received no consideration. My next step was to get a loan through the Small Business Administration (SBA). They had me jump through a bunch of hoops and I had to take one of their courses in small business. The course was pretty good and I was assigned a mentor who told me only one out of ten bars/restaurants make it through their first year and out of the survivors, only one in ten make it to their second year. Defying the odds never intimidated me before so I accepted the challenge and forged on. Part of the training was doing a business plan. I kicked out a real nice business plan and when it came time to apply for grants and loans, I was told I did not qualify. I was not a minority or female business. Back to the drawing board.

On the fencing scene, I was gaining great success and finally heard back from the Army. They declined my application to train. They said I did not have enough experience, even though I always placed higher than their fencers in major competitions. Once again – back to the drawing board.

Activity

I remember the loss I felt when my dreams of a promising career with county police were dashed and the Army had no faith in my fencing ability. After the crushing oppression of the trial, these new goals were like an injection of positive psyche into my soul. I felt excited and energized. Then the county job did not pan out, the Army fencing deal did not pan out, and now the pub deal was looking bleak.

Your activity is to write down goals you had that met opposition. Write down what actions you took afterwards. Did you rework the problem or did you just give up? Are there any patterns you can identify? Are there any changes you wish you had made? Remember the purpose of this exercise is to free yourself from living in regret. Sometimes you have to walk away from something and it ends up being a good thing. Other times when you walk away, it comes back to haunt you. That is what we want to avoid.

En Garde: Crossing the stream of life

Chapter 13

A Tale of Two Pubs

It was the best of times; it was the worst of times" or so wrote Charles Dickens in A Tale of Two Cities©. As I mentioned, my plan for the pub was stalled. I desperately needed the plan to get unstuck. I fell back onto all the lessons I learned and shared in Touché. I took all the elements of the goal apart and started reworking everything. I started meditating and started envisioning myself behind the bar waiting on customers. The imagery became more and more realistic every day. I was able to find a lease where a donut shop went out of business, just south of the Michigan line. The rent was reasonable and because it was in the county, I was able to generate an inexpensive liquor license. While doing my research, I made contacts in the health and building departments who really helped me. I was able to take out a small personal loan for some used restaurant equipment from a restaurant that went out of business. The pieces of my plan were coming together. With some help from my parents, who kicked in some money, and the help of some friends and family for the remodel, I finally had the pieces in place. The remaining piece was the hearing for the liquor license. I prayed hard before the hearing. I prayed for God to have the license denied if this was not the path I was to go down. The liquor commission said I could not hold a liquor license because I was a county deputy. I replied I would turn in my two weeks' notice if approved. They immediately approved my liquor license. Now the teasing began, because everyone was saying look at the cop who purchased a donut shop and turned it into a bar. That is exactly what I did. I had two weeks to get the doors open and I started the remodel. The days were long and brutal. I had vendors and contractors in and out and I was working around them till the wee hours of the morning. Some friends jumped in and helped down the home stretch. My mom and dad helped hang all the décor late the final night because I passed out on the floor. I was up and had the doors open at 10:00 the next morning. We did it! St. George Pub was now a reality and it looked like a pub in England should look. The place filled up quickly and the exciting buzz was electrifying.

This business would change my life for better and for worse. Because I had to be there all the time, I had to sacrifice my fencing and my career ended while competing in a circuit event to get points for the Olympic team. I learned a lot about customer service and working with employees. I sponsored two dart teams and we became the champion of the league. I met some wonderful friends that are still friends today. It was also a lot of fun. It was long hard days, but enjoyable. The freedom of being my own boss was very rewarding.

With that freedom of being the boss also brought the weight of responsibility. It was always financially stressful. I had to generate enough money on the weekend to make payroll and get resupplied on Monday. Then I would have to generate enough money on Monday through Thursday to pay for supplies which were delivered on Friday. In between, I had utilities and rent to cover, along with a thousand miscellaneous extras, which always popped up. I had used every penny I had to get the doors open and had no working capital so I had no option, but to succeed.

These stressors started to impact life with Michelle. I was forced to keep putting my tip money back into the business and I did not collect a paycheck. This created tension in the relationship. Working long hours only added to the problem. My drinking was the last straw. She had given me ultimatums before to quit drinking or she would leave. I would quit drinking, and she would leave anyway. This led to my own insecurity in the relationship which, in turn, fueled more drinking. After months of ridiculous stress from every direction and exhaustion, the sleeping disorders that originated in the Army and the physical arthritis pain from the work I did in the Army caught up with me. I was popping ibuprofen like candy and self-medicated with alcohol to deal with the pain and insomnia. Basically, I would just pass out. It felt like I died every night and was resurrected every morning. I got home from work one night and Michelle was waiting. She told me she'd had enough of my drinking and wanted a divorce. I was pretty broken by this time so I was actually relieved. I cannot say I blamed Michelle because she had her hands full with the kids. The last thing she needed was an alcoholic husband to tend to as an errant school boy. Michelle went through with the divorce, but luckily I was able to see the kids often. They would spend Saturday and Sunday mornings with me at the pub. I would cook them breakfast and they would help me get set up for the day. Then we would play soccer or some other games. Those were great memories. I was frustrated because even though I was part of the problem (perhaps, most of the problem), I was not the entire problem. I felt obligated to tell my kids my side of the story because I did not want them to hate or resent me. Then my mother gave me some great advice. She told me to never speak ill of Michelle because she was the mother of my children and was a great mother to them. Mum said the kids do not need to know your side of the story. Even if they resent you now, they will work through it when they are older. She also warned me that if I did speak ill of Michelle to the kids, they would resent me forever. As much as it pained me to bite my tongue, those words of Mum were pure wisdom!

I started dating someone new and she asked why I drank so much. I responded with a long list of stressors and said if she had all of those problems she would drink too. I was starting to have trouble with exhaustion so I started mixing an energy drink with vodka. I would show up to work in the morning and fire up the kitchen. I would be falling asleep at the bar during my chores so I would have an energy drink with vodka. It would give me some zip. After the lunch crowd left, I would have two more before the dinner crowd came in. After dinner, it was time for dart leagues and the energy drinks had my body just vibrating so I could not hit a thing. I would just slam a couple of pints of ale and the shakes went away and I could play again. After closing, we would go to a friend's bar and have a few more cocktails to celebrate getting through the day. This went on until I hit rock bottom and crashed.

My family was gone, my house was gone, my car was repossessed, and my pub was fighting for its life. My girlfriend went to my parents and told them I needed help. The next morning my mother and Father Andy (my uncle's brother was a priest at Notre Dame) picked me up and they had an intervention. I was furious and started walking back to work. They picked me up on the road and said they could run the business for a few days, but I needed to go into detox. I was so absolutely exhausted that I saw no other option. I knew I could not keep surviving this way. While in detox something special happened. The obsession to drink was lifted. Now I thought to myself, OK now I am sober, what about the rest of my problems? While in detox, I slept a lot, but the only thing I craved was my English Earl Grey tea. Guess what God sent? An English girl was in detox too and had a ton of tea. Every time I smell my hot tea before I drink it I go straight back to that soothing calmness which came with each sip. I remember the first healing sensations of sobriety.

After detox, I went into an outpatient program for alcoholics and started attending meetings. They had us write down answers to all of these questions about what we wanted our lives to look like. I drew a blank. I was so broken, I had no clue what I wanted. I just wanted the suffering and pain to stop. In the outpatient program, they told us only two of the 50 in the class would make it through their first year without relapsing. That caught my attention. Give me impossible odds and I will take that challenge. I decided right there I was going to be the one to make it. They provided a lot of good writing assignments for self-reflection.

During one of the outpatient classes, I was told there was an emergency at work, and I had to leave. When I had arrived, Indiana State Excise Police had my pub locked down. I asked what was going on. They said they received a complaint about having an underage bartender. I did have an underage bartender who went through special training and had a bartending license. They did not cite me for the bartender, but they cited me for the underage worker at the store next door, who had ordered a carryout food order. She returned to get a refill on her soft drink. The police said that there was a minor in a tavern. The police had gone into the cash register and noticed a receipt from the drug store for beer from across the street. The well-intentioned cook saw we ran out of a certain brand of beer so they took money out of the drawer and purchased some across the street. They did not know it was against the law, and were shocked it was bootlegging. It is a stupid law anyway, because you are actually paying tax on the beer twice. These drug stores would buy a truckload of beer at a discount and sell it cheap to get people in their store. The beer distributors would sell it to retailers for sometimes $8.00 dollars more per case than what I could buy it retail. Regardless, the excise police issued me two citations. I contacted the excise prosecutor and brokered a pretty good deal. I paid a $200.00 fine, and if I had no further violations, they would be expunged from my license.

My girlfriend's ex-husband contacted my mother and told her all sorts of nasty things because they were in a custody battle. My mother said she did not want my girlfriend around and told me to leave her behind if I ever came over for holidays. I was new to sobriety and needed all the support I could get. Even Michelle was eventually supportive and we stayed friends to co-parent the kids. My mother was forcing me into a decision I did not want to make. I had to cut the apron strings and go my separate way. My mother and I had always been super close and this pained me deeply. I was told early in sobriety, when you quit drinking every relationship changes; for better or for worse, they change. I was shocked with this change, but felt obligated to hold my ground.

Early in sobriety, I was also told about burning bushes. It references God talking to Moses through a burning bush. These alcoholics would share these stories of how they were in some impossible situation, in their sobriety, and a miracle solution would present itself, which was so farfetched it had to be a miracle from GOD. Hence, the burning bush. The pub was nearing its one year anniversary, and the health department and liquor licenses were coming up for renewal. That was $2000.00 and the judge from the divorce ordered me to pay $1000.00 to my son's school and did not give me credit for all of the child support I had not paid through the county clerk. They did not have pay by phone or online then. You had to physically go to the clerk's office and pay it in person. It was easier just to give Michelle the money directly. I should have known better. The judge gave me one month to pay or I was going to jail.

I thought to myself, how am I going to come up with $3000.00? I went back to the basics I learned in college and grabbed a pen and paper, got quiet, prayed, then meditated. Soon ideas popped into my head and I wrote them down. Once again, it worked! I would have a karaoke contest with qualifiers being selected every week and in the third week, the final contest would be the grand finale. But before the grand finale, I would have a silent auction party, where I sold tickets, and customers bid on items which the beer companies donated. Karaoke night was packed for the first two weeks, the silent auction went great, and the grand finale was awesome. When I counted out the profits, I made $2500.00. I paid the health department and the liquor license, but was still short by $500.00. I only had days left before I could pay the school to avoid jail time. I once again prayed, and the only thing which came to mind was, your prayer has been answered. I was at a loss and the lunch crowd was sparse that day. Then in walked a gentlemen who ate at the bar. He did not say much, other than he liked the place and enjoyed his food. He paid for his food and sat there. He looked at one of the licenses behind the bar and asked if that was me. I said yes. He pulled out his checkbook, and wrote me a check for $500.00 and said, "God told me to give this to you," and walked out. That my friend is a burning bush! The hair on the back of my neck stood up because I just witnessed a huge miracle manifest itself in my life!

St. George Pub beat the odds and we made it through our first and second years. The plaza down the street contacted me and said they wanted me to rent a space twice as big for $500.00 less a month if I moved into their plaza. I did the math and this could be a huge improvement. I could redesign some things I was not happy with and the extra seating would be a huge revenue increase. We were moving! The money was tight but we came up with a plan to relocate. It would mean closing for several months to remodel and transfer the license.

I had made it through my first year of sobriety! I was one of the two out of that class of 50. I also remember the writing assignment I wrote about how I wanted to see my life in sobriety. I was hopeful about my future and wanted to learn how to play cello and paint watercolor. I also married my girlfriend and finally decided it was time to head back to church. I talked with a Catholic priest and was told I could go to Mass, but I could not participate in the Eucharist because I had divorced and remarried. He recommended an annulment for my marriage to Michelle. That did not make sense because I was more than half the problem and she would always be the mother of my children. An annulment would be like we were never married. That did not make sense either. I understood the Catholic Church's rules, and I clearly was operating outside of what they required, but I was looking to be an active member in a church, not just an observer. I followed the lessons learned in college and was quiet, prayed, and meditated. The message was to look at my history. I went through some materials GG had given me. Our ancestors were originally Catholic, but eventually converted to the Church of England. I looked up Church of England and it gave me the number to an Episcopalian Church. I called the priest and made an appointment with him. We felt like it was a good match for us so we started attending church. I told that priest about the hardships I was having getting the second pub opened. He gave me a great nugget of truth. He said if you can accomplish a task which is easy, it is hard to see if God had a hand in it. If your task is impossible, you do not see a way to complete it, and you succeed, then you will see the hand of God working. That thought has stayed with me since.

The priest was right. We successfully opened the Red Lion Pub with a live band and a huge party! It was another miracle! It was the second British invasion! The adjustments to the pub worked well and we started rolling. It was also cool because we would pick up the two eldest kids from school and they would come to the pub, do chores, and do their homework before I fed them dinner. I had a great customer, Renee, who was able to find me a used piano. She would give me lessons every week for two pints of ale. This was my first dabble in music since college, but it helped me heal. I started giving my daughter piano lessons.

Right when it seemed like the world was good, I heard a rumor our plaza was going to be demolished for a grocery store. I contacted some acquaintances on the zoning board. They confirmed my worst fear. My friend Mike had been through a similar situation with his business and the new business gave him money to move his business. I also contacted a local grocery store chain that also provided negotiating tips. I attempted to contact the landlord, but he was unresponsive. The developer would not return my calls either. Something shady was going on.

When it rains, it pours. My grandfather, Richard, with whom I was so close growing up, was disappointed in me when my mother and I stopped talking. His wife passed away and I tried everything to spend time with him. I offered to pick him up and feed him lunch while we watched a game, but he would not budge. I made my amends to him and he still wanted nothing to do with me. The phone rang and it was my mother. She said my grandfather was dying and I had to get to the hospital. I rushed to his room and joined Michelle and Mum. We circled around his bed and prayed. During our prayer, he passed away. We never mended our relationship and that hurt stayed with me. During the funeral, I read a psalm and started crying uncontrollably. I was a mess. Following the funeral we all went to his house where Father Andy held a mass. All of my aunts, uncles, and cousins were there. My Uncle Jeff took the bull by the horns and said this rift between my mum and me needed to stop. We both broke down and hugged each other. The cold war was finally over. My grandfather had a pool which was a family focal point every summer. I went out to the pool and said, "Grandpa, this dive is for you," and jumped into the pool with my clothes on. To my surprise, everyone in the family jumped in after me. It was a very healing time for the entire family.

Activity

In this chapter, the ebb and flow of some major life changes appears. It starts with a fresh start which turns sour. It covers a change in careers. It covers divorce and remarriage. It covers alcoholism which turns into sobriety. It covers the closing of one pub and the opening of a new one. It covers going from one church to another. It concludes with the death of a loved one, and the healing of a friendship. Life is about ebb and flow and learning from our mistakes. I could think back to every situation above and find some valuable lesson I needed to learn. Things became less about good and bad and more about what I could learn from these events. In sobriety, I had to learn entirely new coping mechanisms that ended up being much healthier in the long run. The unique aspect of this chapter is the huge amount of change which occurred in a relatively short period of time.

Your activity is to write down lessons you learned from both the positive and negative events of your life. Remember the only thing we can truly control is how we react to what life sends our way. Documenting your responses may help you grow towards healthier reactions.

Chapter 14

A String of Burning Bushes

The developer finally met with us and offered us nothing. He stated he gave the landlord a quarter of a million dollars to relocate all of the businesses and we should negotiate with him. The landlord told me to negotiate with the developer. I made a reasonable request from the landlord based on the information I received from Mike and the local grocery store chain. They laughed at it and said I would get nothing. I finally told the developer that I invested all I owned into this business so I would lose everything, and if I lost everything, he would never get his store open and he would lose millions. Soon afterward, there was a public hearing at the zoning board for their project. After they made their presentation, I remonstrated against them and exposed their hardball tactics. I reminded the board I was a small veteran-owned business and asked them if they wanted a grocery store in their county that treated small business owners so poorly. The grocery store's attorney got up after me and made all sorts of inaccurate claims about me. He viciously attacked my character. The board tabled the proposal until the next month. The news media actually came through for me and really helped get my story out. I exposed the developer every chance I could. I obtained a copy of the meeting minutes and highlighted the attorney's comments about me. I attached copies of evidence that disproved every allegation made against me. During the next meeting, I gave the board members copies of my packet and pointed out the developer's attorney made untrue statements about me in a public forum for the purpose of getting his proposal passed. I said, "Gentlemen this is the very definition of slander and defamation of character." I asked if their attorney can stoop to this level, to what lengths will they go to get their project completed. The matter was tabled again.

With all the news coverage about the plaza closing, people stopped coming in because they knew we were eventually going to get forced out of business. We scurried to find another location, but nothing was panning out. The landlord tried starving us out. He quit removing trash, emptying the septic tanks, and plowing the snow. He was a Detroit lawyer and a real piece of work. One thing was clear. If I gave up, I would walk out of there with nothing. My only hope was to hold on for dear life to stay in the fight. Slowly I had to start selling off pieces of my restaurant equipment to keep the doors open. The utilities were complete jerks to deal with. They gouge commercial accounts and they were always quick to cut your service. I received a notice stating I had to pay a huge amount to avoid my power getting turned off. Somehow, I came up with the money. Days later, I walked into a pub with no electricity. I called and asked how many times I had to pay in a month and got the run around. I was so mad I filed a complaint with the Federal Trade Commission (FTC). I was on the verge of a panic attack. I played a silly little pity party for myself and yelled to God, I got sober for this? I went behind the bar and poured a pint of my favorite ale and set it on the bar. Then, I starting thinking through what would happen if I took that drink. My early sobriety was rough because it was one emergency after another to deal with. On the positive side, I was no longer hopeless and learned a new confidence: God would take care of me. This time I'd had it up to here. I called Mike, and said, "You told me God would not give me anything I could not handle, and I have had it up to here." He said, "You have a roof over your head, you have food in your stomach, you have gas in your car, and your business is not closed yet. Therefore, you have everything you need for today." He explained God will never give you more than you can handle in a 24-hour period of time. That was an epiphany moment right there. I immediately felt better and the phone rang. It was the FTC, who said I was correct in my claim and they demanded the power company come out and restore service, which they did. The problem was resolved. I made sure I got a good night's sleep and things became more bearable the following day.

In church, a representative from a food charity gave a talk about their missionary work. I only had five dollars left to last me until payday, but I donated it to them and did not think much of it.

Business was hardly trickling in when the landlord filed an eviction notice against us. We went to court and the senile judge decided to go off of the landlord's interpretation of Michigan law instead of Indiana Law. We had one week to vacate the premises. I worked like crazy trying to sell off the rest of our equipment.

We were moving into a townhouse in Michigan, and needed money for car insurance and to renew our license plates. It was our last day in the pub and I still had some tables, chairs, a cooler, and the exhaust fan left. The phone rang and it was the food charity group. They thanked me for my contribution and asked if I had any prayer intentions. I told the woman I needed to sell this stuff to be able to afford rent and car documents until I could find a job. She said a prayer with me and we hung up. The phone immediately rang again and it was another restaurant who wanted my items. We negotiated a price and I told them they needed to hurry. They showed up quickly and retrieved the last of everything. The phone rang and it was the food charity again. They asked if I was okay and I told them about the burning bush miracle I had just witnessed. I said after I paid all the essentials, I only had $20 to last me until I found a job. We prayed again. We hung up and I started to make another phone call. The phone line was dead. Then the lights went out. This gorgeous pub was now an empty shell. I walked out of there with nothing. I turned around and read a Bible scripture where Jesus tells the fig tree to wither up and die. I then prayed that this place would no longer bear fruit. Twenty years later, the plaza was bull-dozed and has sat vacant ever since. The grocery store never built their store and their closest store went out of business. I have no idea what happened to the landlord who cheated all of the businesses out of their relocation money.

We moved into our townhouse and some friends brought over some groceries. Another burning bush! Then the church called and said another parishioner needed help with his business. I called the other parishioner who told me to start

Monday. Another burning bush! I prayed to God, asking how this last $20 was going to make it two weeks until I received my first paycheck. The phone rang and a buddy who managed the Knights of Columbus said he needed help bartending a huge party on Friday and asked if I could cover it. Another burning bush!

Activity

Like I have written before, God is a show off! If He were a quarterback, He would wait for it to be fourth and long in a losing game and throw a touchdown pass to win. This chapter concludes my experiences with the pubs. During this time, I lost everything and regained even more. I went from raging alcoholic to a sober man, learning new coping mechanisms. If I had never gone through these ordeals, I would have never witnessed those strings of burning bushes which so clearly demonstrate God's hand working in my life. For an alcoholic, this was a lifesaving demonstration. I knew God could get me through anything at this point in my life.

Write down a list of positive things which came out of what appeared negative at face value. There are some rich lessons to be learned from situations like these. These are the experiences which build our trust in God's plan for us.

En Garde: Crossing the stream of life

Chapter 15

Stuck

I started work at the parishioner's business. It was a little factory for building electronic brake systems for trucks. It was not hard work and the pay was barely enough to keep the wolves off the door. It was a relief having a steady, predictable income for a change and to only have to work 40 hours a week. I was very grateful for the opportunity.

After a year at the factory, I started to get this gnawing sensation. I knew I was more than this. I did not feel challenged at any level in my life, and it was defeating, knowing I would never get ahead financially. I wanted more out of life, but did not know how to get there. I needed my current income and job security to provide for my family, but could not risk losing what I already had. Remember, I had already lost everything leaving the pub.

I tried to scratch this itch by throwing myself into other projects. I started becoming more involved in church by being an usher, acolyte, lay reader, and started getting involved with the music. I found the writing assignment I wrote leaving the alcoholism program, where I discussed what I wanted my life to look like and noticed that learning cello was on my list. So, I purchased an inexpensive cello and started taking lessons. The cello is a very difficult instrument to learn because there are no frets, but its rewards are worth it. I was hooked. I figured if I could not excel professionally, I could work towards excelling in other areas. That worked for a while, but it was like putting a band aid on a sucking chest wound.

By the second year, I was stuck and did not know how to get out of the rut. Then one day, I was quiet and thought back to my days trying to get into Notre Dame. There were times when I was stuck there, as well. I remembered how I got unstuck back then and asked myself how I could apply those lessons in the present time. I started applying the lessons I learned at Notre Dame and was doing my daily prayer and meditation on my way to work. I envisioned myself not working at the factory. The images became extremely realistic. When I got to work, my boss called me into his office and he said he was going to have to lay me off. He said I did good work, but that I needed to find something more satisfying. On top of that he paid me for the day, and gave me a nice little severance package to tide me over. I was extremely grateful and thanked him. I was free! The sense of relief I felt was exhilarating. I went right back to that bucket list I wrote, and noticed it included watercolor painting. I went to the art store and purchased the materials I needed and taught myself to paint.

On the other hand, my wife was not too happy. She was worried about money and what job I would get next. I tried to explain how God just answered a huge prayer and how important it was to me. She only focused on my finding a job. I tried to reassure her God would not save me from the fire by throwing me in the frying pan. She was skeptical.

A few days later, I went to a meeting and one of the members who owned his own contracting business asked if I could help him with a remodeling project. Of course I said yes and started the next morning. By this time, I had a few years of sobriety under my belt and had seen, firsthand, God providing for me when I could see no solution. I enjoyed going home that evening and giving the ye of so little faith speech! I savored that particular I told you so.

The remodel job was fun and I must have done good enough work because my boss gave me a raise and asked me to work full time. He then told me to learn how to finish drywall from the finishers he had hired. They were unreliable and he would use me for drywall finishing instead. After I completed that task, he gave me another raise and promoted me to carpenter. We did it all. We built houses, did remodels, and replaced roofs. It was hard work, but I learned a ton of trade crafts. It paid better, which definitely helped.

Activity

Everyone gets stuck in the rut, sometime in their life. They even have a name for it called midlife crisis. It is easy to get complacent and allow our lives to plateau. Let's face it. People hate change. Change for the good or change for the worse; it does not matter. It is scary and it can be a lot of hard work. The first lesson I learned in this chapter was that I already had the solution from working previous problems. Those are the skills I used to get to Notre Dame.

The second lesson is when God placed me on a new path, how did I react? I reacted by learning every little task given and becoming proficient at it. I was rewarded with more tasks, which in turn provided more money. It was kind of the karate kid/wise mentor approach: Focus on doing the little things correctly and then they will fall into place to make a larger picture. Even though I had not reached a job which totally fixed that gnawing in my gut, I was able to get unstuck and learn some new skill sets which would come in handy at a later time.

Your activity is to write down times you have gotten stuck. Then, write down how you got unstuck. So many times in life we make it through some daunting task and forget how we negotiated it. This list can act as a "go to" guide for when you get stuck in the future.

Chapter 16

The Unthinkable

During this period of my life, I spent a lot of time mending my relationship with my mother. We had always been so close before reaching that impasse when we did not talk for over a year. During that time, she had no idea about my process of staying sober or the spiritual growth I had been through. We also discussed religion and our views on God. It was a pleasant learning experience for both of us and our relationship healed. As I had learned, when you quit drinking, every relationship changes. I was grateful my relationship with Mum had grown stronger than before.

One day, I returned home from work and my wife was waiting. She informed me she was not happy, had found somebody else, and wanted a divorce. I looked at that relationship as an opportunity to improve on the things I got wrong in my marriage to Michelle. I felt like I did a pretty good job overall. But that is not what she was looking for. I was crushed and the embarrassment of being a failure was over powering. My friend Mike told me to start going to more meetings and recommended counseling. The counseling was very helpful. He started off by telling me my wife did not want to reconcile and I needed to work on some red flags I missed. He also helped me work through Elisabeth Kubler-Ross' five stages of grief. Every week I was given a new writing assignment.

I have mentioned over and over about these writing assignments. There is something magical when we write things down. It helps us plan and identify ideas and concepts we need to learn. I learned this when I was a kid trying to find my purpose, and I still utilize this practice today.

This was the biggest tragedy I had to deal with in sobriety. It was like combat testing a weapon system. You do not really know if it works until it is tested under fire. I had to learn a lot of new coping mechanisms in sobriety and this was the gut check. With God's help, the new lessons I learned held up under duress. This gave me great faith; these concepts could endure any situation. It also strengthened my relationship with God because I could feel Him close as I went through this entire ordeal.

I knew winter was coming and I needed to prepare for the carpentry business to slow down. I went out and got a job waiting tables at night. Every day, I would work as a carpenter, rush home, shower and then go wait tables. The nice thing was that I had weekends off to spend with the kids and my parents.

As winter approached, my mother started having back trouble and went to the chiropractor, who sent her to a medical doctor because there was no problem with her back. We had a wonderful Christmas. Mum worked her magic to have everything just so! Shortly after Christmas, the doctor advised her she had lung cancer and it spread throughout her body. She had quit smoking three years before, and the doctor said she had maybe three years to live. This news was devastating. My children were super close to her, as well. And my dad? She was the center of his world. We were all losing one of the most important people in our lives. She did not make it three years; by mid-February, she was in hospice. I thought to myself, this cannot be real. We just fixed our relationship and now she is leaving. She and my dad were planning on moving to Florida to retire. This was not fair. But, I had to put my pain aside so I could comfort my dad and kids. She was always a hard core Catholic church goer and she honestly believed in heaven and an afterlife. This was her opportunity to put her money where her mouth was because she was living/dying with it. As I sat next to my mother when she was dying, the weirdest thing happened. It was as if we were somehow emotionally connected. I could sense everything she was feeling. I could almost see what she was seeing and hear what she was hearing. It was surreal. I remained quiet and tried to keep tuned into what was going on. What she was seeing was bright and comforting. It soothed and comforted her. She became very peaceful, then just slipped away. The connection stopped. I believe to this day she was giving me a glimpse of heaven.

Activity

In this chapter I was forced to deal with the loss of two important people in my life. Divorce happens to a lot of us and death happens to all of us. I was fortunate to have a strong support system which helped me through. Remember, God likes to work through people in your life. I would have never considered counseling on my own. It was a recommendation from a friend. That counseling was an effective tool that taught me some very strong strategies, which in turn got me through the death of my mother. With that positive experience with counseling, I was able to recommend it to my father, who benefitted greatly from it. This chapter is not all about doom and gloom and loss. It is about bonds with those we love. Those bonds with loved ones can provide hope and faith.

Write down the names of those people who make up your support system. After identifying them, write down some things you would like to remember about them. We all go our separate ways eventually, and it is nice to have those reminders of the people for whom we are so grateful.

Chapter 17

A New Plan

With the death of my mother due to lung cancer, I made the decision to quit smoking. It was a filthy, very expensive habit and I am embarrassed to admit I ever smoked. The truth of the matter was that I did not want to put my children through what I just went through. I had wanted to quit smoking when I quit drinking, but it was not recommended because they wanted me to be successful in sobriety first. It was good advice. I devised a plan to quit within one week. I smoked half the cigarettes I had smoked the previous day, until I reached Saturday. On Saturday, I went cold turkey and it was a rough day. I thought I was going to lose my mind. Sunday was a little better, and Monday I was exhausted. After the first three days, it got easier each day. By the end of my first year, I was disgusted by smoking and could not believe I ever smoked.

I grew up in the restaurant business and waiting tables requires a special skill set. You need to have excellent customer service skills, have thick skin, hustle, and be able to prioritize your trips in and out of the kitchen. I feel like everyone should serve their country in some capacity and I think everyone should have to wait tables, as well.

But then there was the downside to waiting tables. Here I was, this 40-year old man who was hustling tables and just got promoted to bartender. I was waiting on Charlie, Coach DeCicco, and other people, whom I held in great regard. It was embarrassing! I went from Notre Dame All-American, Army officer, and state trooper to waiting on tables. Then I waited on a classmate from ROTC who was flying generals and admirals around. On one hand, there is no shame in doing whatever it takes to provide for your family and meet your financial obligations. On the other hand, I was a 40-year old failure who missed the boat of opportunity. This was a choking mouthful of humble pie. That gnawing in my gut became uncontrollable.

My dad recognized what was going on and had a heart to heart chat with me. He said I needed to get back in my original career field of law enforcement because it was the only profession where the gnawing in my gut disappeared. He explained the importance of being able to get 20 years in to be able to get to retirement. I knew he was right and started working the plan we devised.

The biggest problem was my age. Most Federal law enforcement jobs have a mandatory retirement age of 57 and you need to have 20 years of service to retire. There were some exceptions and waivers, but they were hard to come by. Local police agencies had policies where I could not apply after 36 years-old. I continued to pursue every option I could find and I was hitting a brick wall. I persisted.

Activity

When your stomach keeps gnawing, it is relentlessly trying to tell you, you are on the wrong path. You can try distracting yourself with other activities. You can use obligations as excuses. The bottom line is the gnawing will continue until you get started on the path you are supposed to be on.

Write down what is gnawing at you. Next, list your ideas for making it stop. Somewhere in your writings a plan for getting on the correct path should present itself.

Chapter 18

Run for Office

The quest for finding a law enforcement position was failing to yield any fruit. My age was a constant disqualification. I reached a point where it seemed like an impossibility. I went through Plan (A), Plan (B), Plan (C), etc. Nothing was panning out. It was time to hit the drawing board.

I then came up with the idea, I would run for office. I met with some "like minded" individuals and met someone who was running for Congress, and another who was running for state representative. They suggested I run for state senate. I tossed my hat in the ring and got to work. My thinking was, even if I lost, I would be able to make some contacts who could help me find a law enforcement position.

There is a lot of hard work which goes into campaigning. First, you need to figure out who is who and who does what.

Then you need to find meetings to maximize the number of participants who could hear one of your "stump" speeches. Those were quick speeches, less than five minutes, to sell yourself and platform. My constituent area was three counties big so I had to get the schedule for every city, county, or township meeting. Then you had to get in as many parades as possible. I also spoke at local philanthropic clubs, political functions, and picnics. I had to write letters to the editor and opinion pieces for social media. I had to design campaign flyers to hand out. This brings us to going door to door. Every day after work, I would find an area and go door to door. On weekends, I would go to events and follow it up with going to individual businesses.

It was ridiculously busy. I started dating someone new and she was supportive of the time I invested in the campaign. I picked up volunteers on the campaign trail who helped with treasurer and appointment setting duties. My kids were always helpful handing out flyers and candy during parades. I am not going to lie; it was a lot of fun meeting new people and sharing my ideas. We even had a debate which went great.

There is a dark side to campaigning though. My friends and I were not part of the establishment and the establishment did not appreciate our rocking the boat. We were not their "chosen" candidates, and they never let us forget it. The state party would recognize our opponents at functions and conveniently forget to introduce us. They would take our flyers and hide them. They would steal or cover up our yard signs. My opponent would take my ideas and use them in his next speech for himself. The list of petty annoyances goes on and on.

Then it got even darker. The more name recognition we received, the more aggressive they became. Then the character assassination began. They were using my shooting incident against me and were exaggerating what truly happened. Finally at a picnic, I called them out on it and it quieted. In the meantime the opposite party contacted me and gave me some very damaging information to hit my opponent back. After a lot of prayer and thought, I decided not to use it. It was a dirty bomb, and more than likely the wind would change direction and I would end up receiving the most damage. I also did not want to lower my integrity by playing their dirty game.

I did not have a lot of money but I was able to do the most with what I had. We were coming into the last two weeks before the primary so I took time off work to campaign full time. I would go to businesses during the day, and house to house in the evening. I was doing phone interviews while driving from place to place. It was nonstop, full-tilt boogie heading to the finishing line. Then the threat came. I was told I had better win the primary because if I did not, I would lose my job, like the last person who bucked the system. They warned me that I would probably have to leave the state to find work. I was already committed and there was no way I was backing down now. Mysteriously, I was hit with threatening mail from the prosecutor's office stating I owed child support. Convenient timing! Especially when I did not owe it. The local police removed my campaign yard signs and cited me for having long grass, which had been cut a couple days prior. I was ticketed at the beach for parking without a pass, which was clearly affixed to my windscreen. I was ticketed for having a "For Sale" sign in my vehicle while it was parked in front of my house. Each time, I had to go to the police department and ask them if it were political and they would void the tickets. It was harassment, plain and simple.

I watched the results on Election Day and I was defeated. I was absolutely exhausted from campaigning and heartbroken by the loss. It is devastating to lose after putting in so much effort. I did notice some patterns in the returns. My opponent spent a fortune on his campaign and each vote cost him approximately $12. I only spent $.12 per vote. I was much more efficient with my money. I was also surprised when they interviewed someone who was exiting the polls. They said they actually met me when I was going door to door. In a three county area, I thought that showed a lot of hard work.

I was publicly a good scout about the election and promised to go door to door campaigning for those who won the primary.

The week following the election I called work to plan my return and was told I was being laid off. The restaurant where I bartended had eventually cut my hours to nothing. Was it a coincidence or was it the threat I had been warned about? We will never know.

Even though I was pretty bitter with the status quo, I went door to door as I promised. I had met the new governor, attorney general, and several sheriffs while campaigning and was hopeful it might assist in a law enforcement position. It did not help. I applied for county or state law enforcement jobs and was told to apply again next year or received no word at all. It was pretty obvious I was being punished for trying to overturn their apple cart.

On the positive side, I married my girlfriend and I had that to look forward to. I had also learned a huge amount about politics and campaigning. It was an eye opening experience.

Activity

Sometimes God sends us down these little side paths to learn skills which may come in handy later. At the time, they do not make much sense, but later you will appreciate having attained that particular skill set.

Write down some side paths where you ended up, and identify the skills or lessons you learned. This information will come in handy down the road.

En Garde: Crossing the stream of life

Chapter 19

Court Ordered into Law Enforcement

With the election over, it was time to pick up all the financial pieces. I had been laid off so I had to file for unemployment. With unemployment, they took half of it in child support and then taxed me on the entire amount. After it was all done and said, I ended up with a third of it, but some money was better than no money.

As soon as I received the nasty letter from the prosecutor's office about child support, I sent them all the documentation and court material they needed because they were unresponsive by phone. They did nothing about it. I received a summons to court because they did not think half of my unemployment was enough child support. I responded with a petition which included all the material I had already provided the prosecutor.

When I arrived in court, I explained the situation to the judge and supplied the documentation proving I was not in arrears. He asked the prosecution about it, and they said they had not had a chance to go through it. The judge looked at me and said my petition was five pages long and nobody was going to read five pages. I explained that he had previously slammed me on petitions in the past for being too short. He did not like that. I always felt like I must have done something to anger this judge when I was a trooper because he was always rude, condescending, and would decide against me out of spite. The judge said he would review the material and would make a decision when we returned for the hearing he set for the next month. He then started berating me for not having a job. I explained the various county and state jobs for which I applied. He said he did not think I was trying to find a job and gave me a form to fill out. He wanted me to document every job I applied for and ordered me to take the first job offered. He said I should be able to find a job flipping burgers somewhere.

I had my work cut out for me. I went back to the basics I learned at Notre Dame and set up a strict daily regimen. Each morning, I would spend three hours researching and applying for jobs. I knew I would more than likely have to attend some sort of academy training so I started working out. I would then shower and go door to door looking for jobs. Once a week I would go shooting in preparation for academy training. I spoke with a human resources manager who suggested getting some fresh training to counter my age factor. That was excellent advice so I started taking FEMA courses on line and I obtained completion certifications I could attach to my resume on USAJOBS. I also spoke with a recruiter who explained how to set up my USAJOBS resume because a computer scores them by looking for key words and if you do not have enough key words, no human will ever see your resume. The first place I applied to was a well-known chain restaurant. I did not get the job. Next was one of the biggest big box stores. I do not know if I were more relieved I did not get those jobs or more embarrassed by the fact I could not get hired there. I interviewed as a parole officer and as armed security at the nuclear power plant.

I continued applying for every police/investigator job which opened on USAJOBS. I started the process with TSA at the airport, but it was only part-time. It got to the point where I was applying for any job at any location in the country. I applied for a federal police officer job for the Navy in Virginia. There seemed something different when I applied for that job. A week later, I was called by the Navy and was ordered to Virginia Beach the following week for testing and an interview if I passed.

The following week I drove to Virginia Beach. It poured rain from Richmond to Norfolk. Once I reached Norfolk, the sun came out and there was a breathtaking view of the harbor. There were SEALS helocasting out of a helicopter and you could see the aircraft carriers in the distance. This place seemed pretty exciting. I found the Little Creek Base (home of the East Coast SEALS), where my testing would be the following day. From there I drove past First Settlers State Park and Fort Story. It was now evening and the cicadas were deafeningly loud. I made it to the great Neptune statue at the beach when two F-18 fighters flew by super low. This place was cool. The following morning, I had no problem with the physical agility test and was invited for the interview. It was a panel interview and I gave it everything I had. I had prepared well, and walked out of there confident I would be hired. I drove to my Uncle Jeff's house near Delaware, and headed back home the following day. I had not left my uncle's house for an hour, when I received my conditional offer. I was thrilled about getting back to law enforcement, but then reality hit. I thought, what am I going to do about my family? This place was 800 miles away. The Navy sent me to drug testing at a local hospital and then sent me to Naval Station Great Lakes, IL for my physical.

In the meantime, it was time for court again. The Judge smugly asked if I had my form and asked how many jobs I had applied for. I responded that I had applied for 120 positions and was going through the process for TSA. I explained I had a job offer from the Navy in Virginia. He said, "Well, I guess you're going to Virginia." I asked what about parenting time with my kids and the Judge responded, "Don't worry about parenting time. You just keep the money coming." He then talked to the prosecutor about my arrears in child support and because the prosecutor never reacted to my original mailing, he did not give me credit for any of that time and said I owed an additional $2000.00. I was now paying for a miscalculation by the prosecutor's office. I was furious. I told the judge I wanted a change of judge. He denied that. I pointed out the Indiana Trial Guide states I have one opportunity during a divorce proceeding and the guide says the judge shall grant the request. It does not say can or might. It says the judge shall grant one change of judge. The judge said he was the head judge and was denying it. I filed an ethics complaint against him and the following year our case was handled by a new judge who was much fairer. That did not change the outcome here. I was court ordered back into law enforcement.

Activity

In this chapter, I cover some basic hardships of life. Life is not fair and it can really be frustrating. Sometimes it feels like we go around thinking no good deed goes unpunished. When that judge said he did not care about parenting time and to just keep the money coming, I was thoroughly disgusted. Yes, mothers are important, but children need their father, as well. In reality, I would never have taken the job in Virginia because I would not have voluntarily left my family. The decision was taken out of my hands so I was free to accept the Navy position. That position was the starting point of a new life for me. Even though that judge was wrong, I was able to turn his wrong into my right. Sometimes, when we are dealt lemons, we have to find out how to make lemonade.

Your activity is to write down times when you were dealt an injustice. Then write down how you reacted. Write down if you were ever able to turn a negative into a positive.

En Garde: Crossing the stream of life

Chapter 20

Life in Virginia

It had been 13 years since I was last in law enforcement. Where had that time gone? It was frustrating because so much time was wasted. I had to change my thought process because I had learned a ton of lessons from the various jobs I held and was able to spend a lot of time with my kids when they were younger. It takes what it takes to get you exactly where God wants you. It was pretty obvious I was being "black balled" back home from my participation in the election. Virginia was a fresh start for me. My uncle and father were in the Navy and the Navy was also a great fit for me.

I reported to the police academy at Little Creek and took it seriously. I had trained hard and prepared well for the academy. They also had a lot of new things to teach me. I kept my ears and mind open. When it was all done and said, I graduated top in my class and was assigned to Little Creek.

After in-processing, we were loaded in vans and dropped off at various gates to work as sentries. While riding there, I started to taste some of that humble pie. I thought to myself, I used to be this great state trooper and I have been reduced to a gate guard. I immediately stopped the pity party. Even though I did not make much money, I was not going to jail. I was making enough to pay rent, utilities, bills, and had $50 left over every pay period for groceries. I reminded myself of the "karate kid/wise mentor" lesson I described earlier. If I concentrated on doing the little tasks well, then I would be given newer tasks which would translate into more money. That attitude has served me well working for the Navy and the Navy has been the best employer I have ever worked for by far.

I remember when I first got to Virginia, there was a forest fire in the Dismal Swamp, which put heavy smoke everywhere. Then we were shooting on the indoor range when there was an earthquake. When we were on the outdoor range, somebody over shot the berm when I was on beach watch and the round zinged by, inches from my head. I was scuba diving at Chix Beach and got into a fight with a six foot sandbar shark. I thought to myself, I have been here two weeks and I have been in a forest fire, an earthquake, been shot at, and fought a shark. I like this place!

I went on to quickly becoming a patrol officer and worked my way up. I really enjoyed the base, the work, my bosses, but especially my friends. I made some great friends there and still enjoy their friendship. I remember during one roll call, the captain was chewing everyone out because someone had screwed up. He said, "You all volunteered to be federal police officers so act like it." I raised my hand when he called on me, I said, "I did not volunteer-I was court ordered here." The

Captain rolled his eyes and walked out. A good laugh was had by all. The sad thing was, I was not joking.

Activity

I was forced to travel away from my family to take a job. The whole court ordeal was not fair and may not have even been legal, but it is what it is. The truth is, it gave me the opportunity I needed to get back in the saddle and succeed. The result was the gnawing in my stomach disappeared. I could take pride in myself and serve my country in the process. I am grateful to God and the Navy for giving me a third chance.

Write down times when you were treated unjustly. Then write down if you were able to turn that negative into a positive. If not write down some lessons you may not have learned had the negative thing not happened. The only thing we can control is how we react to situations.

Chapter 21

Get Me Home

Life in Virginia was a double-edged sword. On one side, I loved my job and where I worked. On the other side, I missed my family. I would fly home every other month or so, or they would visit me. The more time I spent in Virginia, the longer the intervals became between going home. My wife and I could not agree on a location where we could both find jobs in the same area. I continued my strict regimen every day. I would job hunt for jobs closer to home for the first two hours, then I would work out. I would go to work and relax when I got home. I spent weekends kayaking, motorcycling or exploring the Colonial Triangle. Virginia had some really cool historical sights. I tried to stay focused, keep a positive attitude, and be ready for whatever the future held.

Approximately two years after being on patrol, I received a call from Michelle when I was putting my gear in the squad car. She sounded very serious and said she had stage four pancreatic cancer. She said, "You need to find a way to get home to help take care of the kids." I felt like someone kicked me in the stomach. I doubled over in anguish and felt like I was going to vomit. I began crying uncontrollably. A thousand thoughts raced through my head. It should have been me. This is not fair. What about the kids? You are going to miss their weddings and grandkids. My radio went off and I was dispatched to an accident. Luckily one of my friends picked up the call for me. I went inside and told my captain. He set up an interview with our Security Officer (SECO), who promised to get me transferred closer to home.

The clock was ticking and I stepped up my efforts to get home. I applied to the Michigan State Police and Michigan Conservation Police. Even though I included letters of recommendation from the state representative, they replied that I should never apply again. I applied at several local and county police departments, but nothing. The Air Force base nearby ran me in circles. Nothing was panning out. There was a Navy base in Southern Indiana-NSA Crane. I called the SECO there and he said he had to wait until a position opened. I applied when the position opened, but did not make the list because someone with a higher veteran's preference was selected. I was a wreck trying to get back home.

The following year, my SECO and the Crane SECO got on the same page and started my transfer process. It would actually be a promotion. By September, I found a place to live in Bloomington, IN and I transferred. I was given a couple of weeks leave to help the kids with Michelle, who was now in hospice. I stayed at the hospice with the kids throughout that week. On Michelle's last day, she called me into her room with the kids. She told the kids she loved them and that she wished she could stay. She told me to take care of them and to love them. I replied that it was easy. Then she asked all of us not to forget her. She passed away shortly thereafter.

This was the hardest funeral of my life. I snuck outside and broke down crying harder than I can ever remember. I do not know if I was crying because of my kids' loss, my loss, or both, but I cried. It took me a bit to pull myself together. This was not about me. This was about being there for the kids so I had to suck it up. I got the kids through the funeral and made sure they were set up. My oldest daughter had started college and my son moved out on his own. My youngest daughter joined her brother so she could finish her high school. I traveled home on my days off.

Activity

I remember vividly the frustration I felt trying to get home. It was impossible to get there quick enough. The important thing was I made it on time to be there exactly when the kids needed me most. So often in life, we try to control and plan, yet it may not be the same timing or plan God has in mind. The end result is God's plan always seems to be better than our plans. My last thoughts about this chapter concern Michelle's fear of being forgotten. This is a natural fear. When you think about it, we live such short lives. What do we really have to show about it, other than the memories we leave with the loved ones we leave behind?

For this activity, write down times when God's plan turned out better than your original plan. The next step is to write down the names of all of your deceased loved ones. Remember them!

En Garde: Crossing the stream of life

Chapter 22

Life at Crane

It was time to report for duty at NSA Crane, which is one of the largest Navy bases in the world. It is remote and the terrain is rugged but beautiful. The people were great to work with and the pace was much more relaxed than the hustle and bustle of Little Creek. I started off doing magazine checks to learn my way around base. To make extra money I would stay four hours over to help the midnight shift with their checks. I was off on Sundays and Mondays so I would drive four hours home on Saturday after work. Then I would leave in the early morning on Tuesday to get to work on time for the second shift. It was a daunting task, but it maximized my time with family.

There are a lot of people who would have enjoyed the numbing routine of checking magazines all day. I remember driving around thinking, am I going to be doing this for the rest of my life? I kept a positive attitude and focused on the karate kid/wise mentor approach of doing the thing I was provided to do the best I could.

I had completed a couple of the hiring steps for the FBI while I was in Virginia. The written test was insane, but I passed it. I had my stuff transferred to Indiana. I was invited to the Indianapolis FBI Field Office for orientation. It was a great experience, but two weeks later, I was told headquarters would not issue me an age waiver. I saw that coming, but I was starting to feel trapped. Certainly, I had more potential than this.

On the home front, things were stale as well. Being away for so long kind of snuffed out the spark. We went to Europe for a vacation and I hoped our trip would rekindle some electricity. It was a fantastic trip seeing Scotland, England, France, Italy, and Spain, but it was more like platonic friends enjoying the sights. I was beginning to feel stuck there too.

I went home for Father's Day weekend and had a nice time with the kids. The following day, I was doing yard work when my wife came home early from work. She said we needed to talk. She said we are both good people, but this is not working and we need to split up. At first, I started to get angry, but the little voice in my head told me to keep my mouth shut and walk away. I felt like a failure, but more importantly, I felt relief. We quickly got divorced. At this point I gave up on serious relationships and just chalked it up to I was a failure at them, too.

Shortly thereafter, I was riding my motorcycle to work, when the neighbor's unleashed dog ran in front of me. I braked and thought I was going to hit the dog, until the woman jumped in front of me. Then, I had to veer off the roadway and into the ditch. This caused my face to smash into the windscreen and split my face open. The bike landed on top of me. The woman grabbed her dog and ran away, leaving me stuck in the ditch. I managed to crawl out from under the bike, drive it home, call in at work, and drive myself to the hospital, where they glued my face back together. The neighbor refused to pay for any bike repairs and never apologized. It felt like nothing was going my way.

Activity

So many times in life, it feels like things are not going our way. We can feel like we are being punished or just stuck in a rut. Again, this is where the Serenity Prayer comes into play: God grant me the serenity to accept the things I cannot change, the courage to change the things I can, and the wisdom to know the difference. With my career, I had to accept what I could not change. The only decision I made was to do a good job at whatever task they needed me to accomplish. In my relationship, I needed the courage to agree with my wife that it was not working. The result was relief, because I did not have to go through the motions of something my heart was not in anymore. The wisdom to know the difference came from my daily prayer and meditation. When dilemmas popped up in my life, I was able to make better decisions, and part of that was because God was part of the process.

Write down a list of times when you stayed in a job or relationship too long, and explain why you made that particular decision. Next, document times you did not try harder in a relationship or job, and explain why. Are there any clues which could improve your wisdom for the next dilemma which comes your way?

Chapter 23

New Beginnings

I figured I would do some casual dating to take my mind off things and to force me from staying home and having pity parties for myself. I dated a couple of nice women, but nothing exciting. There was one woman I was chatting with online who seemed pretty cool. Her name was Bonnie Jo and she was a school teacher who lived about an hour away. I was in no hurry, so I chatted with her for about a month and she asked to call me. She video-called me, and putting the face with the voice flipped a switch. We talked for a long time and I was so intrigued that I asked her to breakfast on Saturday. She was off on Saturdays and I did not have to go to work until later. We met and it was like getting hit with a sledge hammer. She was beautiful. She had told me she did not kiss on the first date, but I was so excited to meet her I just kissed her. It kind of shocked her at first, but she kissed me back! We had a nice breakfast and I knew she was the one. I never looked back and we are still together. When I met Bonnie, it was like the whole atmosphere of my life changed. Things became lighter and more fun. Work seemed better, and my future seemed brighter. She told me good things were going to happen for us and I believed her whole heartedly.

The work front also started to pick up. I was given more responsibilities and worked three double shifts a week to help cover the day shift. I became part of the training team and became a field training officer (FTO). I started to feel a lot less stuck at work. The kids were progressing well and that pretty much completed the fact that all aspects of my life were in tune.

I had sold my cello following the divorce from my second wife and felt like it was time to pick it back up. I purchased a used/repaired cello and started playing again. I had forgotten how much I missed playing. I started taking lessons and found playing cello helped the arthritis in my hands and helped my concentration.

Bonnie and I went shopping and she stated one store's popular slogan from their frequent commercials and pointed at the jewelry store. She was fishing for a commitment so I called her bluff. I took her in there and had her pick out the style of ring she liked and had her finger sized. She was shocked and we left the store and did not really talk about it for a while. During Christmas, I bought her a ruby ring and I am sure she was hoping for the diamond, but I had a better plan. I secretly bought the diamond ring she wanted and waited for Valentine's Day. I had been very sick, but promised to take her to her favorite place called Story Inn. After lunch we walked out to their barn where they had had a wedding the night before. As she was looking at all the wedding set up, I got on my knee and pulled out the ring. When she turned around, I think she thought I had fallen. Instead, I asked her to marry me. She looked confused, then excited, then started crying with excitement. I asked her if that meant she said yes and she said it did! I could not believe I was getting married again, but I had never felt this way about anyone before.

I kept working the overtime to pay for the wedding. We ended up getting married on the beach in Gulf Shores, AL. It was a lovely service and I played cello for her. I played the Prelude from Bach's Cello Suite Number One. The heat and humidity made the cello sound wonky. I had a board to put the end pin on so it would not sink in the sand. The only problem was the chair started sinking in the sand and my butt was nearly on the sand before I finished. It was awful. I thought to myself, at least I can do the ending well. I did play it beautifully. The problem was nobody could hear it because a helicopter flew over. Sometimes you eat the bear; sometimes the bear eats you. Regardless, it was a wonderful day and we honeymooned in the Bahamas. Bonnie was right. Good things were happening for us.

Activity

The moral of this chapter is to just do the right thing in front of you and leave the outcome to God. Of course I was lonely, but I was not looking for a serious relationship. The result was finding my soulmate. On the job front, all I did was focus on completing every little task I was assigned to the best of my ability. Just like when I started at Little Creek, I excelled whenever I was given a new task, no matter how menial.

Write down times when you were rewarded for doing the mundane things in your life well. Next write down times when you did the bare minimum to get by. Was there a difference between your rewards?

Chapter 24

Navy CID

By now, it was apparent I was too old to be a federal investigator. The police department at NSA Crane did not even have a detective/investigator. The billet for a Navy Criminal Investigation Division (CID) Investigator had been empty for over six years. Then one day, they opened it and I applied. I thought at least I would be somewhat of a federal investigator. For my age, I thought it would be the closest I could get.

This was an incredible opportunity so I studied and prepared well for the interview. The interview board consisted of the base commander, a member of his staff, the SECO, and an NCIS agent. I went into that interview and delivered one of the best interviews I had completed, to date. I sold myself hard and my enthusiasm showed. There were quite a few officers who interviewed, but I was confident the job would be mine. I had used all of the principles I learned in Notre Dame and I was visualizing myself doing that job. Every day I visualized having the position it became more realistic. Now it was waiting time. It took a couple of months to get the results. Guess what? I did not get selected. I was heartbroken, but was a good sport and continued doing my current job proficiently. I was told the reason I was beat out was because the person they selected was a credentialed NCIS Agent when they were active duty. I was puzzled. Any other time I envisioned success this hard, it came to pass. In my heart, I still knew I had the position. It did not make sense. Then, a few days later, I found out the person they selected could not pass their physical fitness test. I received word that I was selected! I immediately scheduled my physical fitness test and crushed it. When I came to Crane, I continued the strict regimen I'd had in Virginia. I spent the morning looking for investigator jobs and then worked out before reporting for duty. That dedication paid off because when opportunity knocked I was ready.

My first day on the job, I had to go help the watch commander on the gate because the day shift crew called in sick. We had to cover until officers from other shifts came in to cover the shift. While on the gate, I received a call of a bullet fired into a building. When I cleared the gate I responded, and at the scene I observed a bullet lying on the ground and damaged drywall lying around. I found where the bullet entered the building. I measured the angle the bullet struck the building and used a compass to determine the direction. I had Small Arms Section measure the bullet and they determined it was fired from a .270 rifle. I plotted the compass direction onto a base map and determined it was fired from a group of houses near base. I called the local sheriff's department to accompany me to the residence and asked to see the homeowner's .270 rifle. He asked how I knew he had a .270 rifle and I held up the evidence bag with his round in it. It was determined someone who used his rifle at the range overshot his berm and the bullet came to rest in the building. I had the mystery solved before lunch. I was off to a great start. I continued to build relationships with commands on base, outside agencies, and NCIS. I worked with NCIS every opportunity I had. I built some great friendships.

I served in this position for over four years and loved every minute of it. They treated me great and I received three commendations, including Officer of the Year. I figured this was as close as I could get.

I also advanced in my cello playing and started taking lesson from a graduate student who was obtaining his PhD in cello at Jacob's School of Music at Indiana University. Those lesson sessions were intense and I was able take my lessons on the cello platform that was used by the world famous cellist, Janos Starker (1924-2013). What an honor that was. I continued progressing and Jacobs School of Music started hosting classes for adults to play in a local orchestra. I met some fantastic people there and it was a wonderful learning experience. All areas of my life started to blossom again.

Activity

How many times have I mentioned in this book about doing the mundane little things in front of you to the best of your ability? I have also discussed preparing yourself. It is very hard to stay motivated to search for your goal and work towards it. In my case, I had to keep looking for investigator positions and had to work out to prepare. You never know when opportunity is going to knock, so you need to be ready when it does.

Write down times when an opportunity knocked and you were not ready because you did not prepare. Next, document the times where you did prepare and where ready for when opportunity knocked.

Todd Griffee

Professional headshot (courtesy of Emma Jane Photography)

Chapter 25

Finally Made it to the Big Leagues

I explained how I used my CID position to network with other agencies to better perform my job. I particularly liked working with NCIS because our jobs were so similar. One day I received a report of a lumber contractor getting crushed by a tree. NCIS investigates all deaths aboard Navy installations so I called NCIS. I was fortunate enough to be asked to assist with processing the scene and writing my share of the report. It was a fantastic learning experience that tested my knowledge. It also let NCIS know they could rely on me when needed.

This mutual respect and trust led to making friendships. I became great friends with Jim, who was an NCIS agent. We worked on all sorts of stuff together and he was a fantastic mentor. He was preparing to retire, and told me he wanted me to take his place. I said I was too old. How is that possible?

He replied NCIS has investigators who do a similar job as the agents, but are not restricted by age because they are in a different retirement plan. He provided my resume to the NCIS Central Field Office when he retired and moved. I did not hear anything, but kept applying for investigator positions as they opened. I did not make the cut on the first couple of openings so I kept tweaking my resume.

Bonnie and I were on vacation at Porsche Parade when I received a notification; another investigator position opened. Bonnie asked what I was doing and I told her I was applying for a job at NCIS to see if my resume improvements worked. Two weeks later I received a phone call to schedule an interview.

I prepared hard for the interview. I highlighted and tabbed the NCIS Sexual Assault Handbook in case I was asked technical questions. I looked up 35 questions to be asked on the FBI interview and wrote out notes for the answers. I practiced answering the questions with the formula of identifying a time when I demonstrated the skill in the question, explained how my actions demonstrated the skill, and explained the end result of my actions. I also remember an interviewing tip which the FBI gave me: They explained they did not know me, so it was my job to sell myself because nobody else would. It is not natural for most people to brag, but when you are competing for a position, you need to "leave it all out on the strip." I started visualizing me doing the NCIS job. When the interview came, I was relaxed, confident and well prepared. I did great on the interview and received my conditional offer a couple weeks later.

Accepting this position required us to relocate. We had to house hunt and prepare our house to be sold. The timing would be critical, but leave it to Congress to delay the budget and cause a delay. I was supposed to start in October and ended up starting in December. The only problem with this was interest rates were going up and property values were going down. It was a very stressful situation, but we found a nice home. The only problem with it was that it needed to be totally scrubbed, gutted, repaired, and painted. I used a month of leave and did all the work myself.

I reported to the office and everyone was super helpful in getting me situated. I was given a chance to be in the big leagues but I was stressed about proving myself. I continued the karate kid/wise mentor approach of doing every task I was assigned to the best of my ability.

Activity

It had taken me 14 years of applying to obtain the position I wanted. Yes, that is a long time, but look at all of those other jobs I worked and the experience I learned from them. I used the carpentry skills to remodel a home. I used those serving/bartending skills to polish my soft people skills, which helped with networking, working with other agencies, recruiting, and interviewing/interrogating. I used those Navy police skills to have a better understanding of navigating the military's criminal justice system. I used those FTO and instructor skills to become a firearms instructor.

Your activity is to write down lessons or skills you learned from tasks which are sometimes totally unrelated to your main objective. Next, write down ways those skills could assist you in your primary goal.

Todd Griffee

NCIS Headshot (courtesy of the U.S. Navy)

Chapter 26

NCIS Advancement and Touché

When I got to NCIS, it was not enough to say I made it and rest on my laurels. I was driven to learn and become more proficient. I volunteered to assist coworkers and volunteered for many special details. I did not have much time before retirement so I wanted to make the best of my time with NCIS. I went to work with the moto, if I can help, I will help.

On the home front, Bonnie and I went on a road trip to Yellowstone National Park. On our drive, Bonnie was asking me how I got into Notre Dame, especially with such a unique sport as fencing. As I told my story, she said, "You are writing a book because kids today do not have these goal setting skills available to them." As I thought about it, I remember how I got stuck in my mid-life and used the same principles to get unstuck. I realized those principles work for adults, as well. Bonnie took notes and asked questions the entire time. When we got home, she gave me the notes and I wrote an outline, which I used to write Touché. It is one thing to write a book, but it is another thing getting it published. I've read that only one or two unsolicited books are accepted by a publisher per 100 submitted proposals. You should know me by now. I took those odds and accepted the challenge. Touché was published and it has been an absolute blast doing book signings and promoting the book.

When I was driving on the toll road in my Porsche to attend my first book signing for Touché at the Notre Dame Bookstore, I drove past the now abandoned toll road post. I recalled the anguish I felt in that building years before while I was awaiting trial. I remembered the cruel and callused words of the secretary egging me on to work faster. These memories provided a stark contrast to the miraculous life God had provided. When I was stuck in that building, I would never have imagined being an NCIS Investigator and author, driving his Porsche to a book signing at Notre Dame!

When I look back at the beginning of Touché, the goal was to become a G-Man/federal investigator. Getting into Notre Dame via fencing was only a means to assist me to obtain my goal. Then life happened, and the next thing I knew, I was too old to be an agent. It appeared to be hopeless, yet, by some strange turns of events and a lot of hard work, I was able to achieve my childhood dream. The story I started in Touché has finally come full circle and reached its conclusion. This, of course, was done with the guiding hand of God, who taught me nothing is impossible.

Activity

When I reached my goal, I did not stop. I made new ones to keep improving myself. The Navy has treated me better than any other employer I have ever had. I feel like it is my duty to repay them in kind for the opportunities, they have provided me.

Your final activity is to write a gratitude list. Write down everything in your life you are grateful for.

Conclusion

Like I said in the Introduction, this book is not about what a great guy I am or about the countless mistakes I made. It is about God taking a flawed sinner and making amazing miracles happen in his life. It is a story about getting knocked down so hard I could not imagine a way out of the mess. It is about pain and loss and how God provided the right people in my life to help me cope. It is about understanding nothing is impossible with God. I wrote this book to share my experience, strength, and hope, to share my suffering to bring comfort to fellow sufferers and let them know they were not alone in their pain, and to reassure them there is hope of living a life which is happy, joyous, and free.

When Jesus talks about hiding a light under a basket, He is demonstrating people should not hide their talents and God's good deeds. This is my removing the basket so others may benefit from my struggles. The Bible also commands us to share the Good News. People today are so scared to talk religion that they are embarrassed to even say the name, Jesus. God put a lot of effort into my life to provide me with these wonderful blessings. Please accept this book as my contribution to spreading the Good News!

- Treat every experience as an opportunity to learn.
- Never quit.
- Keep faith that God will provide.
- Know nothing's impossible.

Final Thoughts

2025 started off to be a fantastic year! I was conducting many recruiting events for NCIS, book signings were going well, had a wonderful speaking engagement at a local high school, finished this book, and had the book accepted by the publisher. I completed the FLETC Firearms Instructor Program, and to top it off, I received a huge promotion at NCIS! Things were perfect. But as I have previously written, life happens... The new administration took over and forced the agency to make sweeping cutbacks, which resulted in the elimination of the position to which I was promoted. That was an extremely hard pill to swallow. Simultaneously I was forced to swallow a much harder pill. My primary care physician at the local Veteran's Affairs (VA) clinic found blood in my urine, which required a follow-up CT scan. The scan found a mass in my kidney and the doctors were 90% sure it was cancer. The VA hospital removed the mass.

At face value these two ordeals were overwhelming. Having lost several family members to cancer, it was hard not to imagine it was a death sentence and a rude reminder of my mortality. But when I take a closer look, I can see God's hand at work. I had just finished writing a book about getting knocked down and getting back up. Those lessons were fresh in my mind to keep my focus positive. This was an opportunity for the readers to view firsthand how I utilized these lessons in a recent/life-threatening scenario to navigate these ordeals. On a positive note, the cancer was found early and there was a clean removal of the mass, with minimal chance of reoccurrence. NCIS also did a fantastic job recognizing my leadership skills with an additional collateral duty and being supportive of my surgery.

With all of the criticism the VA health system receives, I cannot thank them enough. From my primary care doctor (with her perseverance and attention to detail), the great competency of the surgery team, and the caring positive, attitudes of the staff, following surgery, I am extremely impressed! What a wonderful group of people.

I invite you to remember the analogy of crossing the stream by recognizing, even though the stones might be slippery or treacherous, God has a path for you to successfully get across the stream.

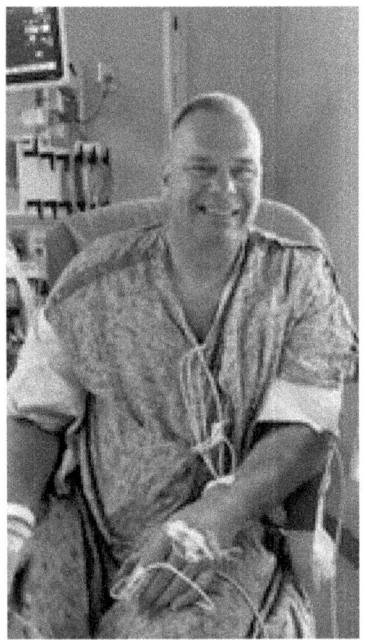

"Day after surgery" (courtesy of Bonnie Griffee)

Prayer

After years of morning prayers and meditation, I devised this prayer. I took some of it from various sources, but it works for me. Feel free to write your own prayer to facilitate your daily dialogue with God.

God, in the name of Jesus Christ your Son, please send Your Holy Spirit upon me to remove all cancer, and this fat. Please remove from me all sickness, illness, injury, and disease, (list additional ailments here). Please remove from me all mental blocks, and musical blocks. Remove from me all jello-brain, forgetfulness, and fatigue. Remove from me all self-centered, self-seeking, and selfish behavior. Remove from me all anger, fear, hate, and resentment. Please remove from me all financial worries, relationship issues, (list your own intentions her). Breathe in me Your healing spirit, and fill me with a clean spirit, a right heart, an able body, and a sound mind. Fill me with faith, love, hope, and charity.

God, please take all of me, good and bad. Please remove from me any defect of character within myself or obstacle in the outside world which would get in the way of Your will, and Your life for me today. That victory over my problems will provide hope to others because if You can work miracles in my life, You can work miracles in theirs. Please do not let me say or do anything stupid today. Please let me do good work, and get through this day.

Thank you God for this beautiful day and the gift of sobriety. Without that gift, I would not have the people, places, things, experiences, and opportunities in my life today.

Holy Mary, please pray with me for my family, friends, coworkers, and their families (Insert names of specific people). Please pray for all who need prayers, all who have passed, all I have hurt, all who have hurt me, all I could be resentful of, and protection from my enemies.

Say a Hail Mary, a Glory Be and an Our Father.

About Kharis Publishing:

Kharis Publishing, an imprint of Kharis Media LLC, is a leading Christian and inspirational book publisher based in Aurora, Chicago metropolitan area, Illinois. Kharis' dual mission is to give voice to under-represented writers (including women and first-time authors) and equip orphans in developing countries with literacy tools. That is why, for each book sold, the publisher channels some of the proceeds into providing books and computers for orphanages in developing countries so that these kids may learn to read, dream, and grow. For a limited time, Kharis Publishing is accepting unsolicited queries for nonfiction (Christian, self-help, memoirs, business, health and wellness) from qualified leaders, professionals, pastors, and ministers. Learn more at: https://kharispublishing.com/

www.ingramcontent.com/pod-product-compliance
Lightning Source LLC
Chambersburg PA
CBHW070155100426
42743CB00013B/2916